Praise for

SECRET STORMS

"A dually narrated, uplifting tale on overcoming profound adversity... Shining through both narratives is goodness and the power of the human spirit."

—*Kirkus Reviews*

"A riveting and heart-breaking but ultimately life-affirming mother-daughter story that defies fiction. Every plot twist, every emotion touches a chord, even for those of us who have not had to endure such a brutal separation. Read it and weep—and then finally rejoice. An ode to the enduring power of family ties."

—Elizabeth Forsythe Hailey, author of
A Woman of Independent Means

"In my writers' workshops, the greatest gospel I can preach is the obvious one—to tell the truth, whatever form it takes. This amazing mother-daughter writing team exemplifies the concept to the max. The plot is Dickensian, rife with villains and struggle, the revealing of it, breathtaking in its simplicity and heartbreaking in its courage. What a story."

—Ernest Thompson, Academy Award-winning
writer of *On Golden Pond*

"What an extraordinary and compelling story, all the more so because it's true—and told so beautifully by its two heroines."

—Alice Maltin, producer & Leonard Maltin, film historian and
correspondent for Entertainment Tonight

"[This] story will break your heart, bring on tears of joy, and make you believe in the healing power of love, forgiveness, and family."
—Meredith Rollins, Executive Editor, *Redbook* Magazine

"This is a story about a love affair—on so many levels. Very unique, very soulful."
—Susan Picascia, LCSW, BCD, psychotherapist and Executive Coach

"I've always known that it takes a courageous woman to give a baby up for adoption, and an even braver woman to tell her story with an uncompromising, raw honesty. Reading this book was like finding the note I'd always wished my birth mother would have left in my file; it shined a light on shaded places in my heart I didn't know existed."
—Kerrin Adrian, Executive Director, BER inc and adoptee

"I can't believe this is a true story... one that will make you cry. And what a happy ending."
—Lynn Pleshette, film producer and literary agent

"Both authors have gripping stories to tell. Readers will delight in their shared narrative, which is as heartwarming as it is engaging... compulsive reading."
—Publishers Weekly

SECRET STORMS

Julie Mannix von Zerneck

Kathy Hatfield

Blue Blazer
2013

Gestational development notes, which close the 'State Mental Hospital'
chapters in Part I, are a medley of facts gathered from various
websites, paraphrased and combined.

An excerpt from "Till There Was You", written by Meredith Willson
in 1957, appears in Chapter 34 'The Vow'.

A portion of this work, edited by Meredith Rollins,
originally appeared in *Redbook*.

Acknowledgements Tree created on www.tagxedo.com

Published by Blue Blazer Productions
Printed in the United States of America

ISBN-10: 0985735805
ISBN-13: 978-0-9857358-0-7

Edited by Aida Raphael
Cover photo by Bryan Hatfield
Book designed by Andrew Jordan

The events, places and people in this book are rendered as accurately as possible, while colored by time, memory and emotion.

Some names and identifying facts have been changed.

Dedicated to the man I love.
-JMvZ

Dedicated to my fathers:
one gave me life,
the other gave me an appreciation of it.
-KH

"The strength of motherhood is greater than natural laws."
Barbara Kingsolver

"If I have learned anything, it is that life forms no logical patterns. It is haphazard and full of beauties which I try to catch as they fly by, for who knows whether any of them will ever return?"
Margot Fonteyn

PART I

Julie

One

STATE MENTAL HOSPITAL

The world will always remember the shots being fired on November 22, 1963 at 12:30 in the early afternoon. But Philadelphia is one hour ahead of Dallas, so for me the event took place at 1:30 p.m. I was in the middle of being transferred from the Psychiatric Institute of Philadelphia, then known as 'a first-class sanatorium for the more prosperous class of patients', to the Eastern Pennsylvania Psychiatric Institute, or, as I got to know it, EPPI, 'a state hospital and home to people ranging from mentally challenged to the criminally insane'.

I was nineteen, blonde with blue eyes, five feet, four inches tall, 102 pounds, and a Philadelphia Main Line debutante. And I was three and a half months pregnant.

"Sit here," I was told by a large man in a stark white nurse's uniform, who was responsible for escorting me from the private hospital to the one run by the state.

I wrapped myself tightly in my wrinkled camel's hair coat and sat on an orange vinyl chair that had some peeling tape covering up slash marks. Peering out through my long veil of unwashed hair, I saw that the waiting room was small, the walls a grimy green. A few feet away, there was an open window smudged with fingerprints, behind which sat two admittance ladies dressed in street clothes. When you have been confined to a mental hospital, even a private one, you don't get to see street clothes too often, except on visitors. In my anger at being there, I had refused any visitors.

An old black and white Philco television was hanging from the soiled wall in a corner of the waiting room. The picture was on, but the volume was turned down low. All four of us heard it, though. All four of us saw Walter Cronkite take off his glasses and state, "President Kennedy died at 1 p.m.... some 38 minutes ago." All four of us—a mental patient, a male nurse and two admittance ladies— heard the news bulletin at the same time.

It was then that I felt a vague stirring in my stomach. Seconds later, a soft flutter, and then a definite trembling. I reached down and covered my belly with my hands and took a deep breath. Up until then it had just been something I had been told about. *You are pregnant. You are expecting a baby. You are going to have a child.* Unexpectedly, in this room that smelled of vomit and floor cleaner, surrounded by strangers, my baby had decided to announce itself for the first time. Suddenly it was real. Something warm burst through me, a kind of euphoria. I sat there in the tight little admittance room and closed my eyes.

This is really happening, I thought to myself. *Oh my God, this is really happening.*

By the end of the third month, all of your baby's organs are present. The arms and legs begin as small buds off the body, and tiny fingers and toe buds begin to form. Even at this early stage, your baby already has individual fingerprints. The genital organs are still forming. Your baby will even move as the muscles begin to function. Your baby has a sucking reflex already in place, and may suck on his or her thumb or fist. At the end of the sixteenth week your baby will be around 3.5 inches long and weigh 1.7 ounces.

Two

BEFORE ME, MY PARENTS

Yes, I was a Philadelphia Main Line debutante, but my parents were not exactly conventional. When my mother first set eyes on my father, he was standing on a sideshow stage, all six-feet-four-inches of him, holding two torches, and great streams of fire were pouring out of his mouth. He was wedged between Daisy the Fat Lady and Percilla the Bearded Woman. My father traveled with the carnival as the fire-eater and a sword swallower in the sideshow, because he was doing research. Later, he would write three books about carny life; *Step Right Up, Memoirs of a Sword Swallower* and *Freaks: We Who Are Not As Others.*

My mother, who was a radio actress at the time, was horrified when her friend pointed out my father, the man she was supposed to go out with that night in between shows. Family legend has it she was not appalled because my father was eating fire and about to down two metal swords set up nearby, or because of Daisy on his left or Percilla on his right. She was totally horror-stricken because my father was naked from the belt up. In her opinion, no polite, well-mannered, civilized man should ever appear with his shirt off in public. In a matter of seconds, my mother turned her back on my father and then all five-feet-two-inches of her walked straight out of the sideshow tent, away from the circus, and went directly home to The Squirrels. Located on Sabine Avenue in Wynnewood, Pennsylvania, The Squirrels was a huge stone home where my mother, her parents, four sisters and four brothers lived.

JULIE MANNIX VON ZERNECK AND KATHY HATFIELD

Later, when my parents had been properly introduced and my father had won over the affections of my mother's parents and siblings with his magic tricks and stories of his exciting carny life—and most probably because he came from a highly respectable family—they fell in love and were married. After that, whenever the carnival came to Philadelphia, some of the sideshow cast would come and stay with us at Sunny Hill Farm, where we were to settle down. Percilla the Bearded Lady, and her husband, Emmett the Alligator Man, and their kids would use the guest room next to mine. And Sealo, a very short man who had arms like a seal, would stay in the other guest room. The rest of the visitors were scattered around, using the attic rooms and the barn and pastures to house their zebras, llamas, trained dogs, and performing monkeys. Because I had known them since before I could remember, it wasn't such a big thing, really, when they arrived, except for the fact that our housekeeper had to iron tons of sheets and fill the bathrooms with the good fluffy white towels that we only used for guests. And, of course, my governess had to neglect me, so she could help my mother in the kitchen. That was just fine with me, because I would gather all the carny kids who were still dusty from the city, climb the pasture fence, and run down the hill to the huge pond at the bottom of the pasture. Hidden from adult view, we would swim to our hearts' delight amongst the snapping turtles, splashing, racing and cannonballing off the wooden raft in the center of the pond into the deep, cool, muddy waters.

***

The money came from my father's side of the family; the

Armstrong Wrights and the Perkinses. John Armstrong Wright, my paternal great-great-grandfather, was one of the founders of the Pennsylvania Railroad and for decades served on the first board of directors. He was President of the Freedom Iron Works near Lewistown and also laid out the City of Altoona, which he later presented to the Pennsylvania Railroad Company as a gift. His granddaughter, Pretty Polly Perkins, was my father's mother and she was just as she sounds: extraordinarily pretty. They lived on Delancey Street in Philadelphia and summered on their estate, called The Hedges, twenty miles away on the Main Line. They were Episcopalians through and through.

My mother's family, on the other hand, were fervent Catholics. Her father and grandfather, both named Jules X. Junker, owned and ran a renowned bakery in Philadelphia. The bakery is remembered to this day, although most people who recall it are all in their late 80s. It was called Junker's French Bakery and yes, they were indeed French. At five thirty every morning, seven days a week, they delivered fresh croissants and rolls, still hot from the oven, in special quilted carriers, to the kitchen steps of every Main Line family of any prominence. In my great-grandfather's day, a bevy of horses and carriages delivered the bakery goods; two decades later an assemblage of white delivery trucks took over. Through the years, all the delivery vehicles were decorated on both sides with JUNKER'S FRENCH BAKERY. It was said that people cheered in the streets when the bakery vehicles drove by.

My maternal grandmother, red-haired Rose Junker, wife of the second Jules X. Junker, was the first woman in the United States to receive a speeding ticket. She was going fifteen miles an hour in Fairmount Park.

Three

STATE MENTAL HOSPITAL

The first few days I was at EPPI, the institute for the mentally challenged and the criminally insane, all that any of us patients on women's ward 'C' did was sit and watch the reports of Kennedy's assassination on television. We all gathered around the small set in what was inaptly referred to as the sunroom. In the Philadelphia Institute, the private hospital where I was kept before being transferred, there had been a real sunroom that had actual sun flowing brightly into it. In this sunroom at the state hospital, you could barely see your hand outstretched in front of you, what with the tight dark heavy mesh that covered the few windows. The sunlight coming into that room could be contained in a small thimble.

Everyone sat on the gray washable vinyl couches and chairs, packed in like sardines, smack in front of the television, watching the scramble of reporters trying to cover this story. By late afternoon, we were told by Walter Cronkite that Lee Harvey Oswald was being held for the assassination of President Kennedy and for the fatal shooting of Patrolman J.D. Tippit.

I didn't sit with the others. I stood behind the couch and chairs to watch the television; it seemed the safest place. In front of me, two-dozen or so unfamiliar people, most of them in shock and suspending their illnesses for the moment, shook their heads, cried and grieved for the loss of a great man.

On my third day at EPPI, Sunday morning, November 24th, Oswald was scheduled to be transferred from police headquarters to the county jail. Everyone was watching the live TV coverage when suddenly we all saw a man aim a pistol and fire at point-blank range. The assailant was identified as Jack Ruby. A stunned silence filled the room. Not even the doctors and nurses who had been sitting with us uttered a sound. Oswald died two hours later at Parkland Hospital. I continued to stand behind the couch and near the nurses' desk, listening, watching and waiting.

On Monday, November 25th, President Kennedy was laid to rest in Arlington National Cemetery. Like the simple turning of a page, when Kennedy's funeral was over and the television networks returned to their normal scheduling, the patients on my ward no longer needed to suspend their illnesses. It began slowly, hardly noticeable at all, quite naturally. A woman with extra-red rouged cheeks began to twirl on tiptoe, humming the music she was dancing to. Some women began to rock up and down, up and down, some rocked fast and some rocked slow. One sat and rocked, another rocked and walked, and others rocked in place and hummed discordantly. A group of four, as though previously arranged, began to follow one-after-the-other-after-the-other, seemingly attached by a single piece of invisible string, around and around the no-sun-room. These were the Zombies—no one and nothing blocked their way, because if anything did it was shoved aside roughly and shouted at. Then, a giant dark-haired woman began to shake the ward with her deep-throated profanities. Stomping the man-sized shoes she wore without socks, her trunk-like legs covered with thick black hair, she roared blasphemies and gnashed her corroded teeth.

I hid in a corner, flattened myself against the wall, and if some-one bumped into me there, I stood by the nurses' desk. I didn't cry.

I did not want to attract any attention. I just stood and trembled and prayed for the day to pass and for God to keep me safe.

These were the same patients who had been sitting on the couch and chairs in front of the television. These were the very same patients who had been crying for the last week. Tears had rolled down the cheeks of these people as they wept for Jackie, Caroline and John, Jr.

In some cases it was obvious why a person was there. But with me, there was nothing you could put your finger on exactly, except, of course, that I had a slight bulge in my stomach. I stood back and watched my fellow patients begin to storm and break out into further uproar. I listened to the echo of their newly retrieved voices bounce hard, back and forth, against one wall and then onto another. My throat tightened. *Oh God*, I thought. My body went rigid. *Please help me*, I prayed. My heartbeat thundered. And then I tasted a sharp acid rising from my stomach. It is an acquired taste, the essence of fear.

The next day, I was taken off the ward for the first time, down in an elevator, along dark, winding hallways and through a door— one of many, each indistinguishable from the others. Inside the room was a desk with a man behind it. The nurse who had escorted me there placed me in a chair in front of the desk and left. The man behind the desk smiled at me for a split second and introduced himself. He was a doctor of psychology, he told me.

I didn't like the way he looked—all one color, with his beige teeth, lips, face, hair, shirt and tie, blending into the bare beige wall behind him, creating the impression that maybe he wasn't there at all. I had to blink twice to focus in on him and when I caught his blank stare it made me so uncomfortable that I quickly looked down at the green linoleum floor. My hands were in a tight fist in my lap. My body was trembling—in fact, I hadn't stopped trembling since the day before. I hadn't slept, either. New noises—night noises—groaning, moaning, screaming, yelling noises filled the ward for the first time since I'd been there. They had kept me awake all night. I lay quaking, curled up in a ball, my back to the wall, my eyes wide open and facing the door so I could see anything that might come through it. I listened intently, concentrating on every little sound, every creak, wondering if it was staying in one place, moving away, or coming closer. I waited for something to happen. I waited for someone to explode. I waited for my door to fly open. I waited for someone to grab me, drag me out of bed and shake me like a rag doll and beat me against the wall. I waited all night, quivering, listening and watching, until the sun came up and the room filled with light and one of the nurses came in for her regular morning bed check.

"I want to talk to someone," I told her. "I need to talk to someone right away."

"I'm told you would like to speak to someone," the beige man, now holding a pencil poised to write, said.

I looked down at my hands in my lap. I took a breath. I willed my trembling to stop.

"There is nothing wrong with me," I whispered. "I shouldn't be here."

"I can't hear you," he said. "Can you look at me?"

"I don't belong here," I whispered a little louder as I forced myself to look up.

He blinked his eyes. He shifted in his chair. He waited.

"I'm not mentally challenged or criminally insane."

He began to scribble.

"I shouldn't be here. I should be someplace else."

"Where *should* you be?" he asked.

"I don't know. Home, maybe." I looked down and hunched over. "Or *a* home. A home for unwed mothers, maybe," I whispered, feeling great shame. A tear splashed onto the green linoleum below and I covered it up with my foot.

"I can't hear you," he said. "Please speak up."

I looked up. "I shouldn't be here," I said louder. "I'm not crazy. I'm pregnant. All I am is pregnant with a child."

He scribbled some more.

"I think I am being punished," I said even louder, wanting him to hear me, needing him to hear me, desperate for him to hear me. "I think they must have put me here to punish me. Because I am not insane." I spoke slowly and clearly, so each word I said was separate and individual and could not be misunderstood.

He kept scribbling.

"I am frightened. I am scared out of my mind here. I am afraid that one of the patients is going to hurt me. Do you understand? I am very fearful for my life here."

He gave no response.

"Please help me," I called out to him. "Please, can't you help me?" I begged.

He blinked his eyes. He shifted in his chair. He waited.

I felt my mouth stretch open wider than my head and my entire body began to quake again. I stood up, put both hands on his desk and leaned in toward him. "Help me. Please, help me," I pleaded, tears of rage flowing from my eyes. "I am scared to death and I need you to help me get out of here."

"Can you hear me?" I began to roar at the beige man behind the desk. "Can you hear anything I am saying?"

After that, I refused to utter a single word. I silently retreated inside myself—a condition that is, I would later find out, called *elective mutism*. If no one was going to listen to me, I resolved, then what was the point of saying anything? I went where they told me, did what they said. But I was stiff and still and silent. Inside, though, I was hot with fury. Enraged. Outraged. Infuriated by what was being done to me.

In the beginning of the fourth month your baby's ear bones begin to harden and he or she may begin to hear sounds. His or her face will be well developed. Eyebrows and scalp hair are beginning to appear. Your baby is now big enough that his or her heartbeat can be heard with a regular stethoscope. At the end of the sixteenth week your baby will be around 5.5 inches and weigh 6 ounces.

Four

I AM BORN

I was an early angel, coming to earth three months too soon, so I was immediately put in an incubator. Fortunately, I had an unusual amount of hair all over my body, so my parents loved me dearly, as though I were their very own baby monkey. But one month later, as soon as I was released from the Bryn Mawr hospital, my high-pitched, continual wailing (not very endearing or monkey-like at all) began to drive both my parents crazy. I'd been brought home to my grandmother's house, where my parents were living at the time. There were lots of people there who could help take care of me. There was my Aunt Aimee, my mother's sister, who lived there with her husband and son, Jules; Anna, my grandmother's housekeeper and John, my grandmother's Japanese cook, who lived in the attic. And, of course, there were nurses who could be hired to tend to me. They named me Jule Hawthorne Mannix. Jule was also my mother's name, so they nicknamed me *Junklet*.

As soon as my parents were able, they were off again traveling, exploring the world, writing and making documentaries about what they saw. They wrote books and articles about their adventures for *Saturday Evening Post*, *Holiday*, *True* and *Life* magazines. It was in their blood. They couldn't help themselves. My parents were masters of flight. They needed to keep moving to stay alive. It was who they were.

My parents came and went from my grandmother's home

regularly. Sometimes I was thrilled to see them and sometimes I did not recognize them at all. Once, when I was four years old, I remember, I went screaming to Anna when a strange lady burst into my room one evening and tried to hug me. Her brown eyes were large with very long lashes and filled with such intense excitement that they terrified me. She was wispy-thin and wore a narrow-waisted tweed suit that was nothing at all like what my grandmother or Anna ever dressed in. Her lips were smoothed in a glossy red that I was fearful would come off on me if she tried to kiss me, so I hid my face behind Anna. Her brown hair was cut short and was wavy and gleamed in the lamplight and looked wild as though she had been out walking in a windstorm. Her nose had a slight rise at the tip like mine and the shape of her face was round like my Aunt Aimee's and her laugh was similar to the sound of bells as my grandmother's laugh was and she felt slightly familiar because of those likenesses—but I had no idea who she was. "Go away," I screamed. "Please go away," I pleaded.

"I am your mother," my mother whispered to me, tears streaming out of her eyes, dripping onto her white silk blouse. Mother or not, I still clung to Anna's apron, shaking with terror.

"Please don't touch me. Please don't let her touch me," I begged Anna. "Please, please, make that lady go away."

My mother was devastated but wisely held herself back. "Don't worry, little Junklet. I won't be going away again for a long, long time. You'll get to know me again. It's going to be all right."

It turned out that one of the reasons my parents had come back to Philadelphia was because my mother had fainted when they were exploring one of the vampire bat caves they were writing about, near Taxco, Mexico. A doctor in Taxco had told her she was pregnant. This was just a few months before giving birth to my brother, who was also several months early. Neither of us stayed in our mother's womb for very long.

***

My mother and father had been living in Taxco, Mexico shooting a short film for Universal, *Hunting Dragons with an Eagle*, that would later be nominated for an Academy Award. For fifty dollars a month, they lived in a rented villa known as Casa Riding that was so big you could ride your horse into the living room. Taxco was a breathtaking place, laced with cobblestone streets, thick bougainvillea dripping from the red tiled roofs of the houses. Their back patio was filled with mango trees and surrounded by a waist-high wall that looked out over purple, rolling hills.

Casa Riding became "sort of an orphan's home for animals," my mother wrote in her book, *Adventure Happy*. They filled the house and patio with animals that had no other place to go and then wrote stories about them; animals like the pair of fluffy baby bear-looking coatimundi, or the floppy but troublemaking kinkajous, who, with their prehensile tails, could turn on the faucets of a sink, stuff the drain with toilet paper, bathe for as long as they needed and then leave the flooding for someone else to clean up. There were also a pair of pet fawns, the falcon, the cormorants; Tequila, a golden eagle; and the star of them all, Aguila, an elegant and beautiful American bald eagle, who had a six-foot wingspan. Aguila, I used to brag proudly, had been in the family longer than I had. In fact, Aguila had lived with my parents in their first apartment in New York City, just after they were married. She used to sun herself daily on their balcony until some officious idiot from an adjacent hotel noticed her and complained. "I am probably the only bride in history," my mother wrote in her book, "who was ever required to train an American bald eagle during her first year of married life."

Because you could exist so cheaply in Taxco at the time, it attracted a lot of artists and writers. The artist William Spratling, who designed stunning, and now very valuable, silver pieces, lived there, as did the writer Saul Bellow, who wrote about my mother in his novel, *The Adventures of Augie March*. They all met up every evening on the balcony of Paco's Cantina, which overlooked the *zócalo*, the village's public square. It was always filled with vendors selling everything from fruits to hand-painted dishes, hats and boots to beautiful sterling silver jewelry.

During their time there, my parents were training Aguila to hunt from horseback. Flying from my mother's outstretched gloved wrist, Aguila would fly across the purple hills and valleys of Taxco, to where my father waited on a nearby hill, also atop a horse, his gloved arm extended, ready to receive the flying eagle. My mother weighed less than 100 pounds. The eagle was a lot for her to cope with, especially on horseback. Finding a horse that could take my father's height was next to impossible. After all, he didn't want his feet dragging on the ground as he galloped over the Taxco country-side with an eagle on his wrist.

And, of course, there were the dragons, the immense iguanas (over twelve feet long in some cases) that wandered the valleys and lay out to sun themselves on the rocky terrain. Aguila had to be trained to descend upon these glorious green beasts, kind of like a helicopter, without having her wings broken by the iguanas' muscular tails. Aguila had to subdue the dragon with her talons without hurting herself or her prey, since the iguanas were to be delivered back to the Philadelphia Zoo. All of this had taken a long time to put together; finding the horses, training them not to shy away when the eagle flew down on them from overhead, training the eagle to fly off a wrist and then return back to it, and then do it again, even when the person with the waiting wrist was on horseback.

***

When Simon and Schuster published *Adventure Happy* in 1954, it was very well received. But it was a strange thing reading about the workings of one's own family growing up. I have always loved reading my mother's book because it's witty and exciting and truly filled with all the amazing adventures we had. But many incidents weren't as humorous from my point of view, as they most probably were to other readers. In a chapter titled "Enter Baby Jule—Exit My Hollywood Career", my mother wrote:

> Dan was in the Navy and stationed at the Photographic Science Laboratory in Washington, D.C. [...] "Jule, I'm being sent to San Pedro in California for a few weeks," [he said one day.] "Why don't you fly there and meet me?" "Dan, I can't," I said amused. "We have a baby now, baby Julie, remember?"
>
> Dan wasn't amused. He said slowly, "Jule, does the baby mean we can't go on anymore trips after the war?"
>
> Ridiculous as it sounds, I'd never thought of this. Dan and I stared at each other. We'd made plans for after the war... another trip to Mexico, perhaps, or to Europe or maybe Africa. We had to make trips to get more lecture material and to do articles.
>
> "Why, this will change our whole lives," said Dan, wonderingly. I jumped up from the table and rushed upstairs. Once in the bedroom I slammed the door and fell on the bed crying as I had never cried before. I had been so proud of our lovely baby and I

was sure from Dan's tone that he didn't want baby Julie...not if she kept us from living the kind of life we'd meant to lead. I'd always sworn that I'd never do anything that would interfere with Dan's life. Now I had done the worst possible thing... had a baby.

In another chapter of *Adventure Happy* titled "Capri Interlude", my mother wrote about the year we spent living on the Isle of Capri so my father could finish a book he was writing about circus life, called *Step Right Up*. They had rented a villa for two hundred and fifty dollars a month that overlooked the three gray rocks in the Bay of Naples called the Faraglioni, where, according to legend, the sirens sat when they tried to lure Ulysses to his doom. My mother described the villa as being "like a marble palace set in a series of terraced gardens an emperor would be proud to own."

She writes:

> I was lucky in having a wonderful French governess for the children. Her name was Lucienne and the children loved her, especially little Danny, who was beginning to pick up French words. In fact, the only words he could speak were French. I was beginning to be worried that he'd never learn English [...] I'd been concerned about sending Julie to school. Fortunately, there was a very nice convent school on Capri where Julie could go. Of course, the school was conducted in Italian but Julie picked up the language astonishingly quickly. Soon, she began to act as my interpreter on the island. I am sorry to say that she didn't stop there... Before we left Capri Julie was talking Italian so fluently that when I spoke to her, she would say in Italian, "I'm sorry Mother, but I just don't understand English."

I really was a handful. Upon our return to America, when I was enrolled in a school in Malibu (where we'd be staying for a year), I kept pretending that I didn't speak a word of English. The school had to hire a translator for me. At that point my poor parents began to plead with me to stop the charade. My head swelled with pride, however, when I overheard them later stifling their laughter in the next room. "That's our little Junklet! She's a real Mannix, isn't she."

Five

STATE MENTAL HOSPITAL

"Why are you here?" a girl with long braids that fell to her emaciated waist walked over and asked me. She was rocking a baby-sized doll wrapped in a stained yellow blanket. I was standing at my usual place near the nurses' desk.

The *why was I there* question was brought up again and again while I was at EPPI. This was the question asked of every patient on the ward and, until it was answered satisfactorily and spread around, no one would quit asking it.

"So?" the girl asked again. She was the first patient on the ward to talk to me.

She seemed about my age—she was my height—but it was hard to tell, since she was so thin and flat-chested. She was dressed in a smocked dress with short puffed sleeves, the kind a girl of eight would wear, if made to. Her voice was gentle, kind, and not high-pitched like a child's would be; but except for her height and obvious maturity, a child is what she looked like. Her eyes were large and round and brown, like the bottom of a deep dark pond. They took over most of her face, which was otherwise very plain. You couldn't help but want to reach over, wrap her in your arms, and protect her. But I would soon learn that to touch her, even to brush by her accidentally, would actually put her life at risk.

"Why are you here?" she asked me again, still gently.

"Shut the fuck up, you whoring cunt," the bulky giant woman with wild dark hair turned around and screamed at her from her seat on the gray vinyl couch. But the girl paid no mind, as though the giant were invisible, and kept talking. "I've been here for three years," she told me. "And I may be here for the rest of my life. It all depends." As she talked, she continually rocked the baby doll in her arms back and forth.

I would later get to know this girl as Theresa. I would also find out Theresa was very firm in her belief that she would not grow up until she found someone to love her. In the meantime, she would remain a child—dress like a child, eat like a child and have horrific temper tantrums just as a child might, but with the force of an adult. After these tantrums, she would sometimes return with a cast on one of her arms, or wrists, or legs, or feet.

***

My room was small, just large enough to hold two single beds and two tall lockers. The beds were white iron and held a single mattress enclosed in thick crinkly plastic, two white sheets, a white blanket and a flat pillow covered in a white case. No stuffed animals or other keepsakes were allowed. There was a single window between the two beds that was covered in thick mesh and the view from it was of a dirt pile and a rusted dump truck that seemed to have been there forever. At least, it was there for as long as I was. The lockers, which stood against the back wall, were locked at all times. If you wanted something from them, like a sweater, you had to go to the nurses' station in the no-sun-room, knock on a glass window and wait for one of them to come out and go with you to your room to unlock them. It was a lot of trouble with very little payoff because you could only keep one set of clothes and a sweater in your locker at a time and nothing else. I suppose the lockers had to be secured so that no one could hide away in them, as I was tempted to do myself occasionally. Of course, there was also the possibility that crude and indecent things could take place inside them, since they were the only hidden space on the ward.

Our hair and tooth brushes and toothpaste were brought to us in burlap sacks bearing our names, every morning and night, so, heaven forbid, we didn't overdose on Crest or Ipana. And I suppose there was also the worry that someone might use the toothbrush to gouge someone else's eyes out, or even their own, in the middle of the night. In the case of my roommate, whom I called The DuPont Executive's Wife, I felt her totally capable of partaking in such an endeavor, which is why I slept with my eyes covered by my pillow every night.

When my roommate wasn't being electrocuted, she walked the halls with the Zombies or she sat and watched me from the edge of her bed with her large lashless bloodshot eyes. You could tell that although her narrow face was drawn and pinched and held no expression at all now, it was likely that she had been a pretty woman at one time, probably very lively, the belle of the ball kind of person who smiled a lot—too much, probably. Now her blonde hair was dull and thin and flat but I imagined that once she had worn it in a shimmering pageboy like my mother and that she had dressed smartly in tweeds and linens. On non-shock days she held herself tall and erect, regally really, so I also imagined that she had been an athlete of some kind, maybe playing tennis every day with a group of friends. Maybe she had even been a Delaware debutante at one time.

Her electroshock treatments usually took place once a week

and when she came back from having them done she was tucked tightly into her bed, where she stayed for the rest of the day and the night, silent and motionless. When she ventured out the next morning, the loose skin on her skeletal arms and legs quivered and her eyes shot around the room like bullets. Sometimes, after the treatments she would talk to me. Well, not talk really. It was more like a ramble; a choppy, abrupt, ramble that hissed out of her dry mouth like snake talk. She always had chapped lips. "Husband," she would splutter. "DuPont." "Clients." "Gloves." "Dinner party." "Lawn." "Cocktails." "So tired." "No." "No more." I could never make total sense of what she said but she did always manage to paint an angry scene with her tone of voice.

The DuPont Executive's Wife and I had meals together the first weeks I was there for no other reason than that we ended up sitting at the same table every time. All the tables were round and beige plastic and screwed to the floor so no one could pick them up and fling them across the room; the chairs were screwed down, too. We didn't linger over our meal, since the food at EPPI was so tasteless it was kind of like eating cream of wheat for breakfast, lunch and dinner; cream of wheat with sugar, cream of wheat with salad dressing, cream of wheat with chicken gravy. We ate in silence except for the occasional words that spit out between The DuPont Executive's Wife's parched lips. "Evening dress." "Garden club." "Grass stains on my slippers." "Help." "No more." "Let me be." I realized very soon that I didn't exist to her. I could have been anyone or anything. I was a shadow lurking on the wall above the bed next to hers. I don't think she could have picked me out if I was standing and smiling at her in the middle of a small crowd of dark-haired Somalians.

Theresa, of all the people on the ward, was the one I felt most comfortable with. It could have been because we were around the same age, or that she was very outgoing and interesting and could talk on and on about anything as if she were a human encyclopedia. Or it could have been that she chose me above all the others on the ward that held twenty to thirty women at a time, to sit with and talk to daily. One day, after Theresa and I had known each other almost two months, she returned from the hospital yet again with another cast, but this one reached from one shoulder to the other. She was wearing a helmet, too, and she had her very own male nurse who stood by her every second now. Unlike other times, where I had just heard about it and seen the results later, I had been with Theresa when she had exploded this last time. As always, she hadn't been angry at the time. She had just been rocking her baby doll, talking to me in her calm, gentle way about nothing in particular, when someone laughing or coughing or sneezing or just reaching out for no reason had by chance touched her. Suddenly, she'd stood up and flung herself against a nearby wall with such force that the room shook. She did this again and again, until four nurses came running and literally lifted her up into the air. Even then she kept fighting. She was a strong little thing, I have to give her that. For someone who weighed no more than ninety pounds, she had the power of an angry rhinoceros.

Despite their various psychological illnesses, as far as I could see, the patients on our ward never deliberately came in contact with Theresa. Even the giant woman who flung herself here and there and raced at great speed along all the corridors of our ward, ranting uncontrollably, was careful not to come close to her. As crazy as we all might or might not have been, it devastated our ward each time Theresa was carried away and returned a few days later, covered in plaster. When she was feeling good, she was as regular and ordinary as apple pie (except for her baby doll and smocked dresses, of course). But when she was feeling bad, which always happened in the blink of an eye, it was terrible; an awful sight to behold. It affected us all and we always went into mourning when they took her away, barely watching television or eating. The waiting was painful because we were so afraid she wouldn't be returned to us, as though we were not deserving of her somehow.

By the fifth month your baby's senses are beginning to activate. Your baby is starting to taste and may respond to some sounds. Its eyesight also continues to develop. Down-like hairs called lanugo have grown on your baby's skin, which help to regulate your baby's temperature. At the end of the 20th week your baby will be around 7.5 inches and weigh 1 pound.

Six

AUNT AIMEE

My Aunt Aimee took care of me probably more than anyone else when I was growing up. By the time her second child was born, she had moved away from my grandmother's place to a home of her own less than five miles away. She kept me during the Christmas and Easter holidays and summer vacations when my parents went on their lengthy travels. She also nursed me through the measles and some very bad influenza. She begged my mother not to put me in boarding school during the week but to let me live with her all the time in her lovely modest home a short walk away from the Wynnewood railroad station. Her husband Sandy worked at the Philadelphia Navy Yard and took the train to work early in the morning and returned by train some time after six in the evening. They had three children by now: Jules, a year older than I; red-haired Rosemary, a year younger; and Alex, four years younger. My mother decided I could go and live with them on weekends and vacations, but during the week I would board at the Sacred Heart Academy in nearby Overbrook.

It was my Aunt Aimee who gave me the only ordinary days in my childhood. Without those times, I wouldn't have known what a normal life was really like. A day at her house went like this: the downstairs grandfather clock would strike. *Bong...bong... bong...* seven times. Good, strong heavy bongs, the kind that make you feel safe in your bed. I was in one of the three upstairs bedrooms, sharing with my cousin Rosemary. Jules and Alex had the second bedroom and my Aunt Aimee and Uncle Sandy had the third. Can you imagine the entire family all on one floor, the same floor, and everyone sharing one bathroom? I was in heaven.

Almost to the second, when the last bong sounded, Aunt Aimee would arrive with two trays, one placed on my bed and the other set on Rosemary's. It was always the same breakfast, every morning: applesauce, a coddled egg, a piece of toast and a glass of milk. And it was the best milk ever in the world, made up from half bottled milk and half powdered milk; the very perfect consistency, I thought. After breakfast in bed, we each took turns using the bathroom to wash up, and then got dressed. Then, for the rest of the day, it was play. Rosemary and I played dolls in the attic; we were both wives whose husbands had gone off to war and we had to take care of the children. We rode bikes in the street in front and visited neighborhood children. On Saturdays, we walked to the local movie theater and threw popcorn. On Sundays, we walked to church and received Holy Communion. We played Monopoly in the basement for hours and left our game set up for days, returning to it whenever we wanted. Every day, lunch was the same: a slice of cheese, a piece of baloney, a carrot and celery stick, a leaf of iceberg lettuce and a glass of my favorite milk. Dinner was usually a piece of chicken, rice or a potato and a vegetable, and one cookie each for dessert. When I was sick and got to stay in bed all day while the cousins went off to school, I would listen to soap operas on the radio with my Aunt Aimee; soaps like "Oxydol's Own Ma Perkins", "Our Gal Sunday", "Lorenzo Jones and His Wife Belle" and "Pepper Young's Family". Later, when the shows were over, I would lie in bed repeating any of the dialogue that I could remember and dream that someday I would be an actress on a soap opera, too.

Those times with Aunt Aimee and her family would become for me the definition of family life.

Seven

STATE MENTAL HOSPITAL

———————

"Fuck that," the giant woman in the back of the room called out. "Fuck that and that and that." Then she took off all of her clothes and ran down the hall.

I eventually named her Mafia Whore. Theresa informed me she had been there the longest. "She never gets visitors," Theresa explained, "but once she told me she has three children, all from different fathers who are all in the Mafia."

It turned out Mafia Whore would make herself my protector in the months to come. She was my bodyguard, in fact. There were some very rough characters on the ward and never once while I was there did any one of them get within a foot of me without Mafia Whore appearing suddenly at my side from nowhere. She never talked to me, never even made eye contact with me, but she took care of me from the moment my baby and I entered that ward on November 22nd until we were finally discharged. I never knew her real name and never understood why she chose to guard me. She was the first of the patients on the ward to recognize I was with child. One morning in my fifth month, I saw her looking at my protruding belly and I sensed a very slight ray of light cross her dark eyes. In a blink, it was gone again.

Mafia Whore was clearly just crazy-out-of-her-mind, what with her constant babbling and sudden massive outbursts, where she would scream out passionately in an unknown language and touch herself in inappropriate places. But she was also crazy-like-a-fox, because at the same time that she was carrying on like a wild banshee, sometimes stripping down stark naked and flinging her clothes wherever she went, she was also fully capable of over-hearing a quiet conversation off in the corner of the no-sun-room, remembering it, and then using it as the subject of one of her babblings.

But there were others like Theresa, whose grief was hidden under the surface where no one could see until suddenly it appear-ed, bold and screaming. One girl in particular, a girl named Dora, seemed very normal and just fine until suddenly she would do some great damage to herself in a matter of seconds. It wasn't necessary for patients like Theresa or Dora to disclose anything about themselves to the rest of us, because after a few days on the ward, any one of us could see they were in immense pain and could be a great threat to themselves, but usually not to others. Dora, for instance, went around with a smile on her face most of the time and talked about make-up and clothes and boyfriends like any normal twenty-year-old. But she did pluck at her hair a lot; so much so, in fact, that sometimes when she came out to breakfast, half of her scalp would be bald. She also plucked her arms and her pubic hair. Depending on the intensity of the plucking, there could also be a lot of blood. It was said that she had tried to kill herself once by spraying an entire can of hairspray down her throat.

Then there was the group of walking Zombies, whom you left alone but were always, and I mean always, aware of where they were so you could leap out of their way as they strode by at a very vigorous pace. Around and around they went, down the hallway where our rooms were, into the no-sun-room, through the dining room, making a U-turn, heading out of the dining room, back through the no-sun-room, down another hallway where another set of rooms were. They would continue back even further to where the two padded cells were, then down again and around again, back and forth, again and again, from the moment they woke up in the morning until they were given their medications after dinner and finally stopped walking and went into a sound sleep, snoring loudly.

There I was, standing silently by the thick meshed window in the no-sun-room and waiting, day in and day out, month after month, trying desperately to feel nothing but affection and love for the baby that was growing inside of me, because I knew that was what he or she needed. If I could give her or him nothing else, at least I could give her the feeling that she was loved. I thought up names. That's what I did all day; I lay on my bed or stared out the window in the no-sun-room and thought up different names for my baby. Parish, from a movie by the same name, was one of them. Then there was Jo, from Louisa May Alcott's *Little Women;* Zelda, Scott Fitzgerald's wife; and Juliana, as in Queen Juliana of the Netherlands. Oh yes, at a certain point, I did decide that my baby was a girl.

I also thought about what I would do with her when she was born. I imagined holding her close and smelling her. I anticipated walking with her, holding her small hand in mine. I thought about what her voice would sound like and the questions she might ask. I began questioning what would happen when she was born and if I would have any say in the matter. No one had told me anything about how long I would be at EPPI. For all I knew, I could be incarcerated there forever. Theresa mentioned once that some of the women on the ward had been there for more than a decade.

I knew I could talk. I knew I could demand to talk to one of the doctors. They would talk to me happily. Every week I was taken to a different psychologist sitting behind a desk. Every week they waited for me to say something for them to write down. All I wanted to do, however, was take one of their pencils and direct it with all my might into one of their eyes. Yes, I could open my mouth and speak to them. I could insist on knowing when I would be released. I could order them to tell me what would happen when my baby was born. But I had already tried all that, and it certainly hadn't worked.

I was strong enough not to have uttered a word for months. And I wasn't going to give up now. Not after all this time. *Damn them for putting me in this position and to hell with them all*, my thoughts raced angrily. But anger is a poison. Holding it in can eat through your insides. Storms of rage began to well up within me. I began to question if that rage had always been there and whether I had somehow kept it hidden. Had these secret storms been burning wild inside me for years? I wanted to rip my clothes. I wanted to fling myself against walls. Sometimes, I thought about opening a vein in my arm and just letting the blood flow out, hoping that all the anger inside of me would flood out with it. A group of Zombies would go by and I'd take off after them. When I got too tired to follow them, I'd sit down on the couch and cover my face with my hands. I rocked myself from side to side. I rocked myself back and forth. *Let them all rot in hell. Let them feel what it's like to be disregarded, disrespected, ignored.* I was no longer the child who needed to please and placate. I wasn't interested in being perfect anymore.

My first time in the confines of a padded cell, I hit and kicked the walls so hard and screamed so loud and wailed so long that when they finally let me out I was weak with exhaustion and had to be helped back to my room. It felt so good to be relieved of all that anger inside of me that I think I was also actually smiling when they let me out.

***

Theresa often lingered with me at a window and Mafia Whore would pass her time just a few steps away in case she was needed. Both of them were aware of the changes going on inside me and they were staying closer than usual. Sometimes two male nurses took a few of us outside for recreation to a caged area where we would walk in a circle with our hands stuck deep into our heavy coat pockets, hot mists of air shooting out of our mouths like we were smoking. Here and wherever else I went, my two friends were always by my side.

I was getting bigger. My arms and legs were thin but my middle was round and bulging. There seemed to be a constant war going on inside of me—one in my head and another in my belly. I was not in the least way in command of what was happening in my belly. It had a life of its own. *Punch, punch, punch,* all the time, even at night, and there was no comfortable way of sleeping. I tossed and turned and got up to pee and then went back to tossing and turning again. But my head was another story. My thoughts began to run rampant, so I had to turn them off, refuse them space. *You can't keep someone in a mental hospital for being with child, can you?* Too much thinking might bring me to my knees. *But let's say you can keep them locked up, then for how long can you?*

As strongly as I fought to keep my thoughts contained, they would occasionally ooze their way out. *Can you keep someone imprisoned until a child is born? Until their born child is taken away because they have been judged legally insane?* And when all this thinking became oppressive, I would fall, fall, fall into a deep dark place that sucked me in ravenously.

And each time I fell into that bottomless pit, I was left suffocated and wasted and lying on my bed staring up at the blank ceiling for days at a time like a stilled Zombie. They were teaching me how to go into another place, these fellow inmates of mine. A blank place that was safe. A mind-numbing place that got easier and easier to find each time I visited it.

But when I left the safe harbor of the zombie mind the thoughts would begin again. *And what happens when I am eventually set free? If I am ever set free. What then? Will I crash into walls forever like a blind butterfly? Will my wings be so torn and ragged that I will be forced to limp through the rest of my life?*

At six months your baby's brainwaves resemble those of a full-term newborn. Your baby is so well-formed that she would likely survive if she were born now. Although her eyes are still closed, she can sense light and darkness. She will probably be at her most active at this time, because she's gaining control of her limbs and she's still got room to move around in. At the end of the 24th week your baby will be around 10 inches and weigh 2 pounds.

Eight

SACRED HEART

I wish nuns still wore habits. There was something breathtaking about the huge long pockets in them that held everything from safety pins to a ticking, man-sized pocket watch to a pen and notebook for writing down demerits. I loved their long black rosary beads, too, the way they swung by their sides as the nuns strode, long-legged, down corridors, and made their swift, sharp turns. I never knew a nun who wandered. There is no such thing as a rambling nun. You could hear their rosary beads clicking together a mile away, kind of like someone tap dancing. The nuns by whom I was taught at the Convents of the Sacred Heart were always addressed as Mother or Ma Mère, never Sister. In this particular Roman Catholic teaching order, a Sister was a postulant, a student nun.

The first Convent of the Sacred Heart I attended was in Overbrook, Pennsylvania, when I was just about to turn six. Rather, that's what my parents told Mother Superior when asked my age on the interview day. "Oh, she is almost six," my mother said casually. In reality, I was going to be six in eight months. Because I was the only first grader to be boarding at the time, my parents made special arrangements for me.

Special arrangement number one was having my very own designated nun, Mother Hunter. Mother Hunter was a very young nun with large cobalt blue eyes, a flawless complexion with a hint of natural rose on her cheeks, and a laugh that was so exuberant she had to cover her mouth to muffle it. All I ever saw of her body were her face and hands, as the long black habit covered the rest.

Her eyes were the first thing I saw in the morning. Pulling aside my covers, she would lead me silently to the far end of the dormitory, past the seventeen other empty white metal beds, to the bathroom, where she would sit me down on a tall metal chair in front of the mirror. Wetting down my electricity-charged blonde hair, she would braid it into two waist-long plaits, as I chatted happily and non-stop to her reflection. She never responded. She wasn't allowed to. Not until she had received Holy Communion and had become one with God, which she did after she got me ready and brought me down to join the older boarders who were already up, dressed and waiting for daily Mass to begin.

A few months after I moved into the Convent in Overbrook, my parents left to go live in Kenya, leaving my brother and his nurse to live with my grandmother. They were writing a book about a white hunter named Hunter (which would later top *The New York Times* bestseller list) and they would have to go on safaris and live in tents, so it might be too dangerous a place for a little girl.

"I'll miss you, my little Junklet," my father told me when he bade me goodbye.

"I wish they had Convents of the Sacred Heart in Kenya," my mother sobbed.

I held on to my Aunt Aimee's hand and cried. "But I don't have to go to school. I can live in a tent and go on safaris, too."

Nevertheless, the plane took off without me.

Once a week I received a postcard from them with a picture of a cheetah or an elephant or a herd of wildebeest. Mother Hunter would always read me the cards during *goutér* (afternoon tea). As I sipped at my glass of milk and munched on my cookie, I listened eagerly as the scrawled ink letters on the cards became words. My favorite postcard was of a Masai woman draped in bright orange, who stared out at me—bold, brave and fearless—with wide dark eyes. She looked so wise. I wanted to be her. I wanted to be this tall spirited woman. I wanted more than anything not to be small with a white face and blonde pigtails.

***

Special arrangement number two was dinner with Father Goodfellow. I sat across the table from him every night, five days a week for the school term. I was too young to eat with the other boarders because my bedtime of 7:00 p.m. conflicted with their dinnertime. Father Goodfellow, on the other hand, liked to eat and go to bed early like me. He lived in special rooms on the first floor at the convent and the nuns took care of him—or tried to. "Father has his own special ways," Mother Hunter whispered to me when she was most frustrated with him. "And there is only just so much we can do."

Father Goodfellow always wore the same thing: a starched white collar, long black vestments and a big silver cross that hung from a chain around his neck. I wore the same thing every day too: a navy blue uniform, navy blue socks and brown oxford shoes. I didn't mind wearing a uniform because it made me feel like everyone else, even though I wasn't. It grew cold early my very first year at the convent, and I remember we both had to wear heavy sweaters in the dining room, though it was only the beginning of

November.

"Mother Hunter, will you please refill my wine glass?" Father Goodfellow would ask. He'd smile patiently, knowing that she would take her time. She always took her time when it came to pouring him more to drink. His thick white hair needed cutting, and it fell boyishly over his eyes whenever he nodded his thanks to her. His wire-rimmed glasses were always smudged with fingerprints and his fingernails were long and sharp and broken.

The table we ate at was so highly polished I could not only see Father Goodfellow's wine glass reflected in it, but also the two silver candelabras, their candle flames, the silverware, the linen napkins in their silver napkin rings, all mirrored twice making it seem each night as though we were at a grand dinner party for more than just the two of us. The bowl of crimson roses always between us in the middle had a sweet scent and were the same color as the fourteen crimson velvet chairs around the table; six chairs on one side, six on the other and one at either end, one for Farther Goodfellow and one for me. He told me that crimson was a holy color. I believed everything he said. I had perfect faith.

When I went away I wrote him a postcard:

Dear Father Goodfellow,

I am on a bot in the midl of the oshun going to the next plase I will be living wich is in France som were. I will miss you.

> *Youre friend,*
> *Julie Mannix, age six and a haf*

***

I was to attend three different Convents of the Sacred Heart before I turned nine: the one in Overbrook, Pennsylvania, one in Paris, France and another in Naples, Italy. This was my mother's way of keeping me close as much as possible when they traveled.

My parents would drop me off with my suitcase and my treasured little red cloth clown. They would introduce me to the Mother Superior, who in turn would hand me over to my designated nun. Once you learned the logistics of a convent, everything was pretty much the same from one to the other. The forbidden nuns' cells were always indistinguishable from each other, with a single crucifix on the wall, a wardrobe chest, a metal bed and washstand. Each of the convents I attended was situated in a magnificent old mansion. Surrounded by luscious gardens, there was always plenty of room for me to run and play. Thousands of hidden mahogany-paneled hallways and rooms filled the interiors of the convents and always there was a sprawling main staircase and one or two side ones that were only for the use of the nuns. And, of course, each convent had a glorious chapel and, on sunny days, a gentle radiance poured in through stained glass windows, filling each place of worship with heaven itself.

All the Madames of the Sacred Heart were dressed the same worldwide also, in those long black robes and white fluted bonnets. And every morning, all over the world, these stately women would form a long, black line and with a graceful, elegant walk they would arrive at Holy Mass just as dawn was breaking. With their hands uplifted and their eyes downcast, they would take to their pews on either side of a flowered altar, and then they would chant—in unison, in a singular voice, the most tranquil voice ever heard. The kind of voice that sounded as though it was coming from one single angel above.

How incredible to belong so thoroughly, I would think. I wanted to belong like that. I wanted to have a voice that would blend in with all other voices. I wanted to be a part of something so beautiful. What if I were kinder and more lovable? What if I were always good, incredibly good, all the time? Then everyone would want me. If I were perfect, all the time, everyone would want me around all the time. And so I tried. I tried so hard. I prayed to God and to all the Saints and to the Virgin Mary herself to help me be perfect. Sometimes, when these prayers weren't answered, I became so wrought with guilt, that I would scream into my pillow so long that my lips would bleed. I was simply a child who wanted more than anything to be a saint. Being a saint, after all, meant you were loved by everyone.

***

Some of my most vivid childhood memories are connected to the Catholic Church. I would put the smell of incense during Benediction at the Convent in Overbrook at the top of my list. Number two would be at the Convent in Paris during early morning Mass, sitting there before breakfast and thirsting after the beads of water that dripped down the sides of the flower-filled sterling silver vases that sat on either side of the altar. Third, (and now that I am thinking about it maybe this should be first) was tasting a precious relic—a piece of Saint Clare's leg bone, to be exact.

I was just turning seven when I did this dastardly deed and was at the Convent of the Sacred Heart in Naples for a few months, having just left the Isle of Capri. On this particular afternoon, there was a mix-up and all the nuns were far away having dinner in their cafeteria, having left me alone in the chapel. That's when I got the idea. Set about five feet apart along the carved mahogany walls were three locked glass doors and protected behind them were the precious relics of various saints. It was my idea, that late afternoon, to test the doors just in case one of them had been accidently left unlocked after being cleaned. I was on my third door when, unexpectedly, it opened. Slowly, I carefully reached in and took out the little relic of Saint Clare. That's when I heard the clicking of rosary beads behind me. Afraid, I popped the relic into my mouth and gently closed the glass door. Picking up a prayer book from one of the pews, the nun smiled at me, and left. Immediately, I took the relic out of my mouth, returned it to the holder and closed the door. But the taste of that holy bone on my tongue remains with me to this day.

***

When I was eight years old, in the fourth grade, fluent in three languages, and back at the Convent in Overbrook, I was given the part of the Virgin Mary in the Christmas Nativity play. Mother Hunter made me a costume out of some leftover satin. Everyone in my class was very jealous. Mary Francis O'Connor cried all through every rehearsal for a week.

"Everyone in my family is coming to see me," she sobbed. "No one's coming to see you. You don't deserve to be the Virgin Mary."

"But the Virgin Mary has beautiful long blonde hair like mine," I told her. "Not short, ugly red hair like yours. And besides, I'm the one who's going be an actress when I grow up, not you!"

Much to my delight, this made Mary Francis cry even more.

The following day, Mother Superior came in to watch our rehearsal. Over the last few years, Mother Superior's eyebrows had turned into one long thick brow that ran across the middle of her forehead, and her laughing days were over as far as I could tell. At the end of the rehearsal, she announced that from now on Mary Francis would be playing the Virgin Mary.

"The part should be played by someone compassionate," she said, "not someone who hurts her friend's feelings." I was instructed to get out of the satin costume made just for me and hand it over to Mary Francis.

"You'll get to play the Virgin Mary next year," Mother Hunter told me as she was getting me ready for bed that night.

"No," I told her. "I'll never play the Virgin Mary and I hate Mother Superior."

"You're too young to hate," Mother Hunter smiled at me with her full sweet lips.

"Well, I do anyway," I said.

"Then you must say a prayer and ask God to forgive you," she advised me as she tucked me in. I said a prayer and asked God to forgive me. *He said He would.*

But several months later the hatred welled up in me again and as much as I tried, it just wouldn't go away. It was a spring morning. Mother Hunter's cheeks were especially rosy when she tied two brand new white ribbons on the ends of my braids, so I knew it was a special day. After breakfast, I went to the fourth grade classroom. It was still empty. I saw that someone had set out a line of folding chairs along the back wall. I went and sat at my desk in the front row, folded my hands and waited as the gentle hush of the nuns' habits sweeping along the corridor outside was replaced by the sharp *click clicking* of high heels and the *jingle jangle* of keys and coins in trouser pockets. It was Parents' Day, but my parents were in Africa again, working on another book.

By nine o'clock, the classroom was full. At precisely five minutes after nine, Mother Superior swept in. We all stood up in unison and greeted her with a heartfelt, "Good Morning, Mother Superior."

"Good morning, fourth grade," she said, "and welcome, fourth grade parents." She looked at the parents in the back and smiled. Then she laughed. I looked up at her, flabbergasted. Her eyes had a twinkle.

"Each child here is a special child," she told us. Her voice was light. Joyful. "Every one of them has something unique to offer and it is our duty, as sisters of God, to assist them in their search for the rare and uncommon abilities that lie deep in each of them."

Dumbfounded, I realized I could see a space between her eyebrows again. She had a golden glow about her, too. Had I been wrong about Mother Superior? Had I harshly misjudged her?

Then Mother Superior reached into the middle of the pile of our weekly spelling tests on the teacher's immaculate and orderly desk. She pulled one out.

"And now we have here," she said, proudly holding the chosen paper up high for our group of visitors to see, "a sample of one of our dear fourth graders' spelling tests."

She was tall and she was holding the paper high over my head but I could still vaguely see red circles around a lot of words. There was a giant FAILED scrawled in capital letters across the top, so I could see that. There was a gasp from the parents in the back of the room. I looked around at my classmates. I looked back at all the parents sitting on the folding chairs.

Mother Superior's face went narrow and her eyebrows attached themselves again. Turning to look at the paper she was holding, her golden glow evaporated. The corners of her mouth fell. Her white teeth disappeared behind her thin straight lips. "And what do we have here?" she asked. "And whose paper is this?"

There was no laugh in her voice now. We all turned and looked at each other. Whose paper was it?

"I don't like doing this," she said, "but I don't see any other way."

Reaching into one of her long pockets, she took out a large safety pin and, in front of everyone, she attached the spelling paper with the giant FAILED written across the top, to the chest of my uniform. It was my paper. The one I thought I had thrown away.

"You will wear this for the rest of the day," she told me.

I could hear the parents in the back of the room move around, but none were mine. I waited for the classroom to empty, then I tried to hide in my locker but I couldn't fit.

"I hate her," I sobbed to Mother Hunter.

"You don't really," she said, unpinning the spelling paper from my uniform with shaking hands.

"I do and I don't care if it's a sin," I said firmly. "I hope she dies. I hope Mother Superior dies in her sleep and that it hurts her a lot."

The following morning when I woke up Mother Hunter was nowhere to be seen. For the first time in my years at Overbrook, she was not there to wake me up. I called out, but there was no answer. I listened for voices but everything was quiet. I finally found everyone in the refectory, three floors below, having breakfast.

"What's happening?" I asked.

Everyone stopped and looked at me.

"Something big," one of them told me. "Mother Superior is dead. She died in her sleep last night."

"You didn't kill her," Mother Hunter assured me as she attempted to pull a wide-toothed comb through my hair later that morning. I could tell from the look on her beautiful face that she was really trying to believe what she was telling me.

"When God wants us, He takes us. No one can wish a person dead."

I caught her blue eyes in the mirror with my blue ones.

"Oh, *I* can," I told her. "And I did."

***

When I went away I wrote Mother Hunter a postcard:

Dear Mother Hunter,

I am on a boat called the Isle de France, in the middle of the ocean going to the next place I will be living. I will miss you.

Your friend,
Julie Mannix, age eight

Nine

STATE MENTAL HOSPITAL

Though many patients incarcerated on psych wards for long periods of time may not be able to control their own feelings, they do seem to have a special ability to tap into and help liberate many of the severe anxieties of their fellow patients. In some cases, they acquire more information on the subject of psychological disturbance than many doctors do after years of study.

For example, I witnessed a group therapy session where a very overweight, gray-haired woman, Hazel, was restored to health by another patient, with only a few simple words. Hazel was one of the rockers on the ward—she rocked from side to side—possibly in her mid-sixties at the time. In this particular group session, the spotlight was put on Hazel, someone so far gone that she was usually ignored. Not only did Hazel rock but she was also a babbler. She babbled to herself day and night. Even in her sleep she babbled. No one could stop her. She was background noise on the ward and if she stopped for a moment to sip at a glass of water, or blow her nose, we would all turn to see what was suddenly absent. "Mary, Tom, Arthur, Sue," she would recite. "Liberace, Liberace, Liberace. Andrew, Joseph, Sally, Nellie. Liberace, Liberace, Liberace." It was Mafia Whore herself who jumped in where no "psych doc" had ever been before. I think Mafia Whore even amazed herself by her abilities that afternoon.

"Fucking cunt, if you shut the hell up once in a while your goddamn son might come and visit you."

The room went still. Total silence reigned. Hazel had stopped babbling and rocking and was looking at Mafia Whore with teary eyes. Then she began again. "Mary, Tom, Arthur, Sue," she mumbled. "Liberace, Liberace, Liberace. Andrew, Joseph, Sally, Nellie. Liberace, Liberace, Liberace."

"If you want your fucking goddamn son to take you out of this crap hole you better shut the fuck up and keep still."

The doctor tried to intervene but Hazel, who had stopped babbling and rocking again, lifted her wrinkled hand to quiet him.

"How did you know I had a son?" Hazel asked the crazy black-eyed Mafia Whore.

"Every fucking one knows that Liberace and his goddamn mother are two fucking peas in a fucking pod."

The room went quiet once more.

"My son is dead," Hazel said in a whisper. "Even if I did stop, he couldn't come and get me out of here."

"Fuck," said Mafia Whore.

"Yes, fuck," agreed Hazel in a hardly-audible voice. From then on she stopped rocking and never babbled again as far as I know.

Sometime later, Hazel was discharged. Rumor on the ward had it that she went to live in a home for the elderly.

***

Recently, I looked up EPPI on the internet. This is just one of the many statements I came across: "I know someone who spent about a year at the Eastern Pennsylvania Psychiatric Hospital and he went through some heavy-duty abuse by staff and other patients. The place deserved to be closed down. It should have been closed down years ago."

At seven months, your baby is growing fast and space is getting tight. Your baby can see and hear now. She is already becoming accustomed to voices, as well as the sounds that are familiar where you live. What you eat can change the flavor of the amniotic fluid, so she is already becoming accustomed to the types of food you eat. Your baby's lungs are preparing for breathing, and her movements give her muscles exercise. There is tremendous brain and nervous system growth taking place this month. At the end of the 28th week your baby will be around 11 inches and weigh 3 pounds.

Ten

SUNNY HILL FARM

Our home, the home I grew up in from the age of nine, was a
wonderful old stone house covered in tangles of green ivy and built
by one of George Washington's generals. Where it wasn't stone it
was whitewashed concrete and the myriad green-paneled windows,
upstairs and down, were bordered on either side by forest green
shutters. Situated in the center of twenty-four secluded, glorious
acres, it was called Sunny Hill Farm. The front door, a tall, solid,
haughty white thing, with a massive brass knocker on it, and a
covered porch in front of it, was hidden behind a five-foot hedge,
so visitors were forced to enter the house from the shed door that
was right there when you drove up the long drive and parked. This
door was green and small. My father had to duck to go through it.

Inside, the house was divided into two parts. A pair of French
doors, which my brother and I had to knock on if we wanted to
enter, closed off the section where my parents lived and worked.
Their part of the house consisted of a huge living room, a large
bedroom, a small bath and the 'little library'. The living room was
filled from floor to ceiling, wall to wall, with four generations'
worth of books. At the far end was a giant stone fireplace, on either
side of which stood my parents' very used and very comfortable
slip-covered chairs. On the mantle stood dark wooden dolls carved
by the Masai and a collection of various Kachina dolls made by the
Hopi Indians, to whom my father sent the eagle feathers they
needed to make these. Around the room were various pieces they

had collected during their travels, such as camel saddles, which they used as side tables or footrests; a massive elephant foot used to hold bottles of liquor; a rhino foot, which held tobacco for my father's pipe; Masai spears, blow guns, a koboko whip and a large boar's head. They kept overflow and first edition signed books in the 'little library'. Their bedroom was where my father wrote and my mother did her bills. Her desk was a small Chippendale, covered with mountains of papers. His was an antique mahogany table with a single drawer where he kept a neat pile of yellow paper and several pencils. The only things on the desk were his black Royal typewriter and a stack of the pages he had written that day. It was my parents' habit, when they were home, to sit in their chairs on either side of the large fireplace in the evening and, as my father read, my mother proofread and edited the yellow pages he had written that day with one of her No. 2 pencils.

The part of the house where my brother and I lived was very friendly. There was the shed, which housed the icebox, freezer, and a long, hanging wood board with hooks on it, where all the keys to the various animal cages were hung. The small kitchen, where my mother made vats of the world's best fried chicken, also contained a long Formica-topped table and two mismatched chairs facing a single window. In the winter, my brother and I could look out and see a family of red cardinals dancing in drifts of white snow while we were having our usual breakfast: freshly made oatmeal with a yellow pat of melting butter on top.

The sunroom was where we kept the piranhas, flesh-eating fish, in giant tanks. The mealworms we fed the piranhas were kept in one of the two basements, the cold one, which was under our side of the house. My brother and I each had a bedroom of our own on the second floor. There were two other bedrooms as well, so if we wanted to change rooms we could, and we often did. There was only one bathroom upstairs, so my brother used the one downstairs near the kitchen (the guest bathroom, as we referred to it), which he often shared with Peter the python. Peter enjoyed bathing in the tub, but, on occasion, wandered annoyingly to the toilet, which most guests did not appreciate. We children had a living room of our own, too, which was dubbed the 'little living room'. It was where we sat on Sunday evenings to watch our one television show a week. It was also where we displayed our Christmas tree.

The Christmas when I was twelve, I received a wonderful baby spider monkey whom I named Jupo. After I opened her crate and let her out, she immediately climbed our Christmas tree and wrenched away most of our beautiful family ornaments. A floor-to-ceiling wire enclosure had to be erected in my bedroom, but she cried when I put her in it at night. Also, it was so cold that winter that all the blankets in the world wouldn't have kept her warm enough because she would just toss them off. She even ripped off the little doll-sized, red-striped pajamas I'd put her in. So, in the end, she slept with me, inside my nightgown, stretched out across my chest, where she could hear the sound of my heartbeat under her own. Jupo only loved me and would cling to me, her arms around my neck, all day long. She kept my life exciting with all of her antics for five wonderful years. And then it was time for her to find a mate, which she did—Butch, a strapping young spider monkey, who lived at the Norristown Zoo in New Jersey.

We had a cheetah named Rani who lay out on my bed some afternoons and slept 'till it was her feeding time. And of course we also had the American bald eagle, Aguila. We had Otty, the otter, who liked to attack me in the pond and nibble my toes and make me scream bloody murder when I was swimming, and Coy, the coyote. We also had several ocelots, a bunch of skunks, vampire bats, a tarantula that we used a toothbrush to clean, six peacocks and pea hens that cried *heeeelp, heeeelp* when anyone drove up our quarter-mile drive; eight falcons, an unattractive hyrax, a fox named Tod, whom my father wrote about in one of his children's books, *The Fox and The Hound*; and many other animals, including dozens and dozens of various snakes, some very poisonous, that came and went through the years. We also raised rats and rabbits to feed these animals. And then there was the roadkill that we found along the country roads. Our icebox in the shed was filled to the brim with not only the usual chicken and lamb chops, but with square enamel trays of dead furry things that had wandered too close to Route 401 just off Bacton Hill.

When I was little and still living at my grandmother's house it was actually safer keeping me inside a cage because so many of the animals my parents brought back had free range; my playpen had a top cover and was made of metal mesh. As a young child, I was not encouraged to have friends for obvious reasons, but later, when I was a teenager, school friends would flock to our house because they were utterly and completely captivated by what they and their parents referred to as "the eccentric Mannix family and their menagerie".

At least once a month there was an article in one of the Philadelphia newspapers about adventurers Jule and Dan Mannix returning from Kenya, or leaving for India, or acquiring a pair of kinkajous, or having just written a new book. I hated when my friends brought cameras when they came to visit and had me take pictures of them with Rani licking their hands.

***

I missed the traveling when we finally settled down at Sunny Hill Farm. I missed getting to live at Aunt Aimee's house. I missed the Convents of the Sacred Heart and the nuns, especially Mother Hunter. I missed being the youngest and all the attention it got me. I missed visiting the small homey hotels in Paris, Rome, and London. I still longed for Capri, where I made my first Holy Communion, and our villa there, that dripped in purple wisteria.

But at the same time, I loved the big old stone house we moved into suddenly one day; I loved its old rickety wood barn and the haylofts for jumping into, its pond for dipping my toes and sliding on in the winter when it froze over. And although my parents continued to travel around the world, I began to experience a sense of stability.

When we first moved to the farm, about twenty minutes from the closest town of Paoli, I longed for someone to play with. But after I began attending Agnes Irwin, a private girls school, where my grandmother Pretty Polly Perkins had gone before me, I acquired plenty of friends; some, in fact, that I would keep for the rest of my life.

The *school train*, as we called it, connected farms to cities, though it was not just for students, but also for men and women headed to work or pleasure. It took us up and down the Main Line of twenty-miles-or-so tracks between Philadelphia and Paoli every day, five days a week. The train dropped us off at our schools' stations in the morning, and then we would walk the half-mile or so through sun, wind, rain, sleet and snow, depending, to our various schools.

Schools named Episcopal Academy, Agnes Irwin, Haverford Shipley and Baldwin were all schools that our fathers and mothers, grandfathers and grandmothers and great-grandparents had attended before us. It was said by many generations and so it must have remained true through the years: Irwin's had the dames, Shipley had the games, and Baldwin had the brains.

We took the train back to our home station again in the late afternoon. Except for our ballroom dancing classes held once a month at the Merion Cricket Club, the train was the only place any of us got to be with the opposite sex. Our favorite conductor on the train, with his white, waxed mustache, was an older gentleman nicknamed Frenchy, whose punch on our monthly tickets was in the shape of a star. We all were very respectful of him, as our parents and grandparents before us had been. The day that Frenchy retired they had to add five extra cars to his train because three generations of riders rode with him that Friday morning. As Frenchy passed down the aisle from one car to the next, to the next, clipping his famous star into each ticket for the last time, no one said a word. Instead, every one just looked up from their copy of *The Philadelphia Bulletin* and gave Frenchy a simple nod of the head.

That is the Main Line for you—very understated; many a word through the years was left unsaid.

Eleven

STATE MENTAL HOSPITAL

"Why are you here?" Theresa inquired of me yet again.

I was over seven months pregnant now. By this point all of the hospital population who cared was aware that I was with child.

Theresa and I had grown to be best friends. We spent every minute we could together and because of that and because I never spoke, our friendship was based on something I was unaccustomed to: intuition and observation.

I had had friends like Christy, Sally and Sydney, all of whom were attending colleges now. Those friendships had been based on the things we did together, like riding horses, talking about boys, and deciding what we were going to do with our lives. I also had Poppy, my closest friend, but she lived all over the world, so sometimes we didn't see one another for a year at a time.

With Theresa it was totally different. It was a friendship of silent faith and equal trust. If we could have slept in the same bed together, on top of one another, our palms spread open and plastered against each other's, we would have. We accepted each other fully.

***

It was dinnertime and Theresa and I were the last two left in the dining room. "So why?" Theresa asked again for the umpteenth time. I hated it when she asked. My guts rolled over and the hair on my body stood up. I hated it so much that sometimes I would have to get up and walk around with the Zombies for a while. Then, of course, Mafia Whore would go ballistic, terrified I would be hurt, so she would have to either follow close behind or act as a block in front of me.

But Theresa chanced asking the *why are you here* question every so often anyway. I knew why I was there. I had known the reason I was there since the second day I was confined to the first mental hospital, the Philadelphia Institute.

But to have the first words out of my mouth, after so long, be ones that explained what had transpired to put me here, was too much for me to take on. And I still needed to bury my feelings. Had I answered, everything in me would have shattered.

I wanted my first words to be ones I would be proud to declare, words that would fill me with the joy of the moment. Little did I know that this was waiting for me right around the bend.

The eighth month is a time of rapid growth for your baby, especially brain growth, so be sure you are eating well. She will gain at least two pounds before the end of this month. Her lungs are still developing, but the rest of her body is pretty well-formed. Her eyes are functioning well now, able to focus, and she even blinks. You may be able to recognize her periods of sleep and wake. At the end of the 32nd week your baby will be around 12 inches and weigh about 5 pounds.

Twelve

THE MONTH OF MAY

By the age of eleven I had figured out that making my own birthday plans was the thing to do. And so, the tradition of inviting my friends Sally, Sydney and Christy over for a three-day sleep-out began.

My birthday event would begin on a Friday afternoon in the middle of the month of May, come rain or shine, and run through to Sunday afternoon. The first thing we would do was set up my parents' old canvas tent in the pasture up on the hill, under a blossoming Hawthorne that overlooked the muddy pond below. We had ice chests filled with eggs, bacon and liverwurst, a cast iron frying pan for cooking, and a wood crate to protect our loaves of bread and bags of potato chips from the raccoons, possums and foxes that came our way in the dark of night. Our four ponies tethered nearby, we had only to reach out to touch their soft doughy noses whenever we felt like it.

Each day, we woke up with the sun and every night we lay flat like pancakes under the stars and talked about our wildest dreams. In between, we went for long rides on our ponies, climbing up the hills to the forest above, where we raced along the winding paths, jumping fallen branches that blocked our way. Nothing held us back. We were brave as thieves, stealing time not intended to be ours. We were kings. We owned it all up there in the forest, secluded from the rest of the world. We would scream out nonsense words like *rah rah racker rah* and *guttersnipe* at the top of our lungs as we galloped along, avoiding low-hung branches by wrapping ourselves flat against our ponies' necks. When we'd reach a spot in the woods where warm beams filtered down through the treetops and found us, we would slide from our ponies, exhausted, and spread ourselves out in the sun, outstretched hands touching hands so that we were all connected. It was there in that safe circle that we confessed our secret hopes for ourselves each year. Mine was always the same. "I want to be an actress," I confessed. "I want to be in movies, I want to be on stage... I just want to be an actress."

Just as the sun was about to disappear, we would mount our ponies again and begin to make our way back along the snaking path through the forest and the shadowy ghost-arms that reached out to grab us around every bend. Shrieking noises overhead and all around propelled us to move faster and faster. We would call out to each other in low, urgent whispers, "Quick. Hurry. Go," our bodies stiff with fear. We had heard rumors—bloodcurdling stories. Four girls grabbed in the woods on a night without a moon. Ravaged. Strangled. Dismembered. Never to be seen again. Or had we made it all up ourselves around the campfire the night before?

Later, we would go for late night swims in the muddy pond, tripping down the hill from our tent, naked as jaybirds, and cannonballing in. We would emerge shivering and shaking with the hairs on our legs and arms standing straight up like sharp pins and then we rolled ourselves dry in the pasture grass and huddled together into a single figure, our breathing yielding and kind, our hearts beating like soft drums in the still of the night.

Thirteen

STATE MENTAL HOSPITAL

I suspect now that Theresa never really expected me to answer her question about why I was there. She had recognized a long time ago that I would never be able to tell her. But she was still not above tormenting me a bit, pushing me to the edge—although, to her credit, she always pulled back in time. It was her duty, as a friend, to remind me that I had some figuring out to do, some digging and delving, some examining of hard facts. She was forcing me to prepare for the day I would give birth.

"Well, why ever you're here, I'm glad, " she said, embracing me with her sweet tone. Then, she looked away, embarrassed. "I wish I were your baby. I bet you would have loved me," she whispered.

And that's when I saw something in Theresa change. Was it the shape of her face, the bend of her body, the rhythm of her breathing? *A flash... A flicker...* Suddenly, a puzzle piece dropped into place, and then another piece, and slowly, I began to see the puzzle start to take shape. A white shingled house with a brick chimney. There was smoke coming out of the chimney. There was a wide-open window, with a curtain wafting in and out, blowing in the wind. I heard a baby crying, the piercing sound drifting out of the window on the wave made by the curtains. The wailing became louder, more and more ferocious. *Attention must be paid now*, the howling demanded. *Now. Now. Now.* Theresa had been that baby; that baby who would not be stilled, because no one had come to pick her up, hold her close, quietly love her. She was alone and always had been.

And then I spoke for the first time in six months. "Yes," I whispered back. "If you had been my child, I would have loved you very much."

I reached over and almost touched her ever so tenderly, ever so lovingly, and my heart went out to her. I actually saw my heart move through the air, go into her, and then leave and come back and reenter my body. And I thought, *anything is possible. Everything is possible.*

In this ninth month, your baby's biggest job is to continue to put on weight. She needs this extra weight to supply her energy demands during the first few days while she is waiting for your milk to come in. Her downy hairs are being shed. Your baby is receiving antibodies through the placenta, and after she is born she will get antibodies through your colostrum and milk. At the end of the 38th week your baby will be around 14-15 inches and weigh about 6-8 pounds.

Fourteen

COMING OUT

Much has been written about the Assembly. Celebrated in society columns, toasted by George Washington, the Assembly has been held since 1748. It is indeed the oldest and perhaps most exclusive annual ball in the United States. It occurs once a year shortly before Christmas. The right to attend the Assembly is passed down from father to son. An Assembly son can continue to attend, regardless of whom he eventually marries, but an Assembly daughter can continue to attend only if she marries an Assembly son. The rules are so strict, in fact, that a particular gentleman whose family had made a fortune during the industrial boom after the Civil War was so disgusted when he tried to get into the Assembly and was refused, that he left his fabulous art collection to the National Gallery in Washington, rather than to the Philadelphia Museum of Art. In short, quoting from the *Philadelphia Inquirer,* "if you want to go to the Assembly ball, you have to pick your parents carefully."

Just imagine: twenty highly bred eighteen-year-old debutantes, hair long and luminous, smiles radiant and gleaming, all dressed in billowy long white gowns and elbow-high white kid gloves, being spun around and around the majestic Victorian ballroom of the Bellevue Stratford Hotel by equally highly bred eighteen- to twenty-year-old gentlemen clad in custom-tailored black tails, white ties, patent leather shoes and also wearing white dancing gloves.

The debutantes and their gentlemanly delights are skipping and cavorting at a breathtaking pace, twirling and twirling, feet barely touching the floor, to a Strauss waltz or maybe "The Merry Widow", expertly played by the Meyer Davis Orchestra. Great-grandparents, grandparents, parents, aunts, uncles, cousins and friends stand inches from the dance floor, wide-eyed with glee, all there to witness and celebrate the year's newly presented and their coming out into society.

After the grand waltz, each debutante steps up alone. Cheeks flushed, arms spread wide, head tilted downward in respect, eyes lustrous with pride, each girl makes a graceful genuflection toward the Old Guard, many of whom were in her place decades before. Sometime after midnight there is a buffet breakfast, more dancing, and then "Good Night Ladies" is played and the elite of the Main Line gather themselves and begin to leave. It is between two and three in the morning and the moon is lowering itself in the sky as it always has, and always will.

Every so often a rather eccentric person can be spotted in the crowd of onlookers at the Assembly: a lady with a warm gray cashmere sweater buttoned up to her neck, worn under her maroon silk strapless gown, and maybe a moth hole in one of the sleeves; or maybe an extremely tall and very handsome man with a trickle of blood on his white tie and gloves. Has he possibly cut himself shaving and it has escaped the view of his wife? Maybe. Maybe not.

The Main Line is notorious for eccentric people who are received as normal. A dowager driving herself up to the Bellevue on the night of the Assembly in an aged and battered car with a ripened camel's hair coat slung over her shoulders covering her quarter-century-old brocade gown could be indeed a Biddle, a Chew, a Pew, a Wetherill, a Wanamaker or a Roosevelt, and worth millions. Some people live out of trunks that belonged to their great-grandmothers. It's the only place of elegance where you can see a few moths flying around.

That man with blood on his white tie and gloves was my father and I was one of the girls twirling on the dance floor that night. I remember sitting in the back of the car, in my billowy gown, on the way to the Assembly that evening. I remember my delicate mother in the front seat, dressed in a magnificent emerald green ball gown, sitting next to my father, dressed in white tie and tails. I remember begging, pleading with my father to please, please not stop on the road, just this once, just because he had found a triple dose of roadkill. But for the life of him, he just couldn't give it up. No matter that he was headed to the Assembly with his daughter who, in the next few hours, was going to be presented to Philadelphia society. No matter that he already had cages of rats and rabbits enough to feed his vast menagerie. He just could not find it in his nature to give the roadkill up even just this once. My mother was to assure me later when I tearfully accused my father of being totally unreasonable that he was not that at all. "He's just being thrifty. It costs a lot of money to feed our animals."

***

I had been preparing for my coming out party since I was ten years old. My friends and I had learned the box step at our first dancing class, 'Thursday Afternoons', at age ten; at age twelve we had learned the foxtrot at 'Friday Evenings'; and finally, at age sixteen, we had begun attending 'Saturday Evenings', where we learned to waltz. We all had been primed for years and years to "trip the light fantastic" and it had finally come to be.

I shared my own debutante party, held on June 16, 1962, with my best friend Poppy Mull. It was a circus. Yes, a real circus, with a giant red and white-striped canvas tent from the top of which flew multi-colored banners that waved and flapped in the cool breeze of that evening. The tent was set up in the back pasture at Sunny Hill Farm. Guests arrived and entered the house by way of the front door. Immediately, they were ushered to the reception line in the living room, where Poppy and I stood next to my mother and Mrs. Mull. After shaking our gloved hands, they were offered a glass of cold champagne from a silver tray held by a clown with a spectacularly large red nose. Escorted by two other clowns with long floppy shoes, the guests were then led out to the spotlighted tent, where the party was to take place.

There was an orchestra and a beautifully waxed dance floor out in the pasture on which we could whirl around and around with our *debs' delights*, handsomely clad in their black dinner jackets. There were magicians, and fortune-tellers, and cotton candy and popcorn. There was also a large circus ring where, for an hour, all five hundred of us, ranging in age from my brother, the youngest at fifteen, to the eldest, Mrs. Pancoast, far into her nineties, stood and cheered Lalea Ray and her seven red-plumed llamas, a dozen dogs who leapt through fiery hoops, a small herd of very elegant zebras and Queenie, the baby elephant.

The following day, pictures of Poppy and me posing with the

red-plumed llamas appeared on the front page of every society section. Judy Jennings, the society editor for the *Philadelphia Inquirer*, wrote, "Julie Mannix and Poppy Mull won hands down for the most unusual presentation party given in recent years. Julie's gold and white sari, brought back from India on one of her parents' many trips there, was worn with an aquamarine and pearl necklace which belonged to her grandmother on the Mannix side (Pretty Polly Perkins)."

"One thousand balloons floated in the tent," wrote Ruth Selitzer, society editor for the *Philadelphia Bulletin*. "We [...] stayed until 3 a.m. It wasn't just a party, it was A Circus."

Fifteen

STATE MENTAL HOSPITAL

The DuPont Executive's Wife was with me when my water broke. It was around three o'clock in the afternoon and I was standing at our window staring out at the pile of dirt and the rusty old dump truck, when suddenly I heard a popping sound and a river of water flushed out of me. I let out a scream. Moments later, everyone was there in the room—Theresa, Mafia Whore, a few of the Zombies, and half a dozen nurses.

"Jesus Christ! It's only your fucking water breaking. Don't you know anything? You're just like the fucking Virgin herself," Mafia Whore yelled.

Theresa stared at me, her huge muddy eyes even larger than usual. Her little girl dress was smudged with purple and yellow chalk. She was holding her baby doll in her arms. "What's happening?" she asked, frightened.

No one knows what causes labor to start or when it will start, but several hormonal and physical changes may indicate its beginning. These changes may include the passing of the mucus plug and water breaking.

Sixteen

THE PLAYHOUSE

After graduation and coming out, I left Sunny Hill Farm at the end of June to join the Gronningsater family at their summer home on Lake Champlain. Ann and Arne Gronningsater had five children ranging in age from four to eleven and I had been hired at fifty dollars a week to take care of them. It was my first job and I loved it.

That fall I would be attending the Neighborhood Playhouse in New York City, an acting school, which I had auditioned for and, to my utter delight, gotten into. At the end of the summer, the Gronningsaters invited me to come live with them in their New York apartment on Manhattan's Upper East Side. In exchange for caring for the children, I was given free room and board. My other choice had been to stay at a hotel for girls, with three girls to a tight little room. I wisely chose the Gronningsaters.

The Neighborhood Playhouse was and still is located in a great old brick building on East 56th Street. From the moment I walked in, that wonderful September morning, I felt like I had finally arrived in the world I had been dreaming about. The halls were filled with tall and short, beautiful and ugly, fat and thin, black and white; students dressed in crazy ways, talking passionately, dancing wildly, and zealous about everything they did. No one cared about how many generations someone's grandparents had been living in the United States. No one gave a hoot about social position of any kind. They only cared about *the moment*.

During my first month at the Neighborhood Playhouse, I was extremely shy and reserved. Everyone seemed so uninhibited and confident, as though they all knew something I didn't. They painted themselves in bright make-up. They swore openly, talked about private things like a guy having a hard-on for a girl or even another guy. They wore revealing clothes: really tight, really transparent, and really short. I tried to fit in, but I didn't have the right equipment. My make-up consisted of a bit of rouge and light lipstick. Language-wise, the word 'shit' was as good as I could give. And clothing-wise I stood out a mile apart in my wrap-around skirts, Peter Pan collared shirts and cashmere sweaters. Eventually, a girl from Greece, who dressed in loose flowing dresses, a Julie also, the daughter of a director by the name of Jules Dassin, befriended me. "I like the way you don't care about being different from everyone else. I am that way too," she told me.

At first, when I had to do a scene with someone, I was so afraid that I could barely talk above a whisper. Of course, no one wanted to work with me. I was always the last to be picked as a scene partner. It was in my improvisation class, however, that I first began to relax. "I am thinking we might do well," my friend Julie suggested, "if we do less talking and more listening." "Yes," I agreed. "Too much talking is very boring." *Alright*, I thought to myself, *I can do this*. No script, no preparation and five minutes at the most were all we had to create a character and a situation. It didn't need to be complicated or funny, we just had to create a world out of nothing. On shaky legs, I got up when it was my turn. Taking a deep breath, I switched off my mind and moved onto the stage. When it was over I was as surprised as everyone else by what I had done. "Good work, Julie," our teacher Hal Baldridge called out when my wordless improv was done. A smattering of applause rustled through the classroom. Julie squeezed my hand. That afternoon I was invited to join some of my class for a beer at Joe's, a local bar. A gathering of actors. I felt so proud to be included. "That was not you up there today," a girl with hair the color of fire told me across the booth we were all crammed into. "When you started to unbutton your shirt and smile like that, I thought, god-damn she's really good."

By Thanksgiving I was beginning to grow as an actress. Finally, the various things I had been learning began to come together and sink in. On some occasions I could forget about acting and fully disappear inside my character. Sometimes I would get so involved in a scene I would look up after it was over, surprised at where I was. When I was put together with scene partners now, they seem-ed pleased. Since my first day at the playhouse I'd been terrified that I might not have the talent to be a good actress. Now I knew that being good was within my reach.

Though the Playhouse was a two-year program, you had to be invited back for the second year. The last weeks of school we all held our breath, waiting for our acceptance letters. When I re-ceived my acceptance in the mail, I got down on my knees and thanked God in the heavens above.

Seventeen

STATE MENTAL HOSPITAL

The DuPont Executive's Wife gawked at the mess on the floor by her bed where my water had just broken. "Wailing in the middle of the night... Invitations... Birthday candles... His secret visits to her in the middle of the night," she ranted. Then... "Only some of us live happily ever after."

I stared down at the floor. I was suddenly scared. Soon my baby would be coming out of me. I would see her. I put my hand over my mouth. *Oh my God*, I thought to myself, *it's finally happening. I'm going to have my baby.*

> Typically, when your water breaks, you will feel a gush of liquid followed by a steady, uncontrollable leaking. It is a good idea to call your doctor at this point, as your baby is more susceptible to infection.

Eighteen

THE MAN IN THE PINSTRIPED SUIT

Now that I had graduated from my first year at the Neighborhood Playhouse, I decided to get a summer job. I convinced two men who would turn out to be friends for the rest of my life, James Hay and David Rawle, that I would work eighteen hours a day, seven days a week, if they would take me on as their apprentice at the Westbury Music Fair in Westbury, Long Island. This was the summer that would change my life. This was the summer novels could be written about. This was the summer of my utter annihilation.

It must have been raining when I first met the man in the pinstriped suit. I was wearing my tan, belted raincoat. It must have been cold, too, since I was wearing my brown leather gloves. It was June of 1963, and we met across a giant tent. He was standing at the entrance, washed in sunlight, and I was standing diagonally across from him, half a football field's distance away. Jim Hay introduced us over the huge expanse, called out our names, *Julie Mannix I would like you to meet Frank von Zerneck*, the introduction echoing through the emptiness. Frank von Zerneck was five feet, ten inches tall, had thick black hair, and was strikingly distinctive in that he seemed filled with a confidence so pure, so evident, that I could feel its force reach all the way across the enormous span and smack me in a deep place somewhere. He stood there, dressed in a blue oxford button-down shirt, dark pinstriped suit pants, and a tie loosened at the collar. His suit jacket was slung over his shoulder. His eyes, even from a distance, were brilliant with enthusiasm, and his smile was filled with the energy of life. I felt like I was melting into a puddle on the cement floor right there and then, soon to be mopped up by Billy, the theatre's one-eyed canvas custodian. It occurred to me for a quick millisecond that my parents had first set eyes on one another in a tent, as well.

***

Frank von Zerneck was the theatre's treasurer. I passed by his box office more than a dozen times a day on my way to and from the office, where I was not very good at working. Actually, hopeless would be a better word. But Jim and David never complained. I came in on time, and was willing to stay way past midnight. My spelling was atrocious, but they were not put off by it and used to laugh, give me an affectionate squeeze, and say, "Our secretary needs a secretary."

One morning several weeks in, I was given the job of addressing and stamping over two hundred envelopes. I worked on the task for a day and a half, careful to write each word neatly, checking each address twice. Then I hastily put a return address label and stamp on each one and walked them over to the post office. It was a nice day and good to be outside. *Not bad*, I thought to myself. *Look what I just did.* When I handed the thick stack to the postman, he was aghast. "This won't do," he told me, his large round eyeballs exploding with red veins. "I cannot accept this. What moron did this, anyway?"

What was he talking about? I had worked so hard. I had

checked everything twice. And then I looked at the stack of envelopes and suddenly saw what I had done. I had put the return address labels on the right side of each envelope and the stamps on the left. I had reversed everything and I had done this two hundred times. I was mortified. A burst of tears swamped my eyes and I shook my head to get rid of them instantly.

I all but ran back to the Music Fair and managed to hold in everything until I was by myself, hidden behind a side of the tent where no one ever went. It was there that I finally broke down and cried, big choking sobs of shame. But it turned out I was not by myself, after all. There was someone right around the corner having a cigarette break, and he heard me crying. Frank stepped around the corner in his dark pinstriped suit and made himself known. He had a white handkerchief. It was clean. It was ironed. I took it and wiped away my tears. He led me to a nearby green wooden bench in the shade of a willow, where theatergoers sat to drink their drinks and talk their talk during intermissions.

He laughed sympathetically when I showed him what I had done. His eyes, his marvelous warm hazel eyes, expressed delight as he told me he thought what I had done was totally enchanting. He shook his head, his black hair gleaming in the sunlight.

He was a problem solver, he told me. He loved problems and he loved solutions. He loved math. He had been very good at math in high school. He loved it so much, he had even tutored other students in the subject, for free, sitting in a booth at the back of Horn & Hardart's Automat on the corner of Broadway and 46th Street in Times Square. He told me he had gone to the High School of Performing Arts, a school for actors, dancers and musicians. When he was fourteen, he had sold cold drinks and programs in all the top

Broadway theatres; he not only made some money, but got in to see all the shows for free. He had been an actor on Broadway and he had also been in many live TV shows, like "Robert Montgomery Presents", "General Electric Theater" and "The United States Steel Hour", to mention just a few.

He had gone to Hofstra College on a scholarship, and after graduating, he and four friends had started a comedy group named The Uncalled Four, and occasionally they would play at Steve Paul's The Scene and other comedy houses for free drinks. When he wasn't acting, he got jobs as a stage manager off-Broadway and also did some stage lighting. This was the first time he had worked as a treasurer in a box office. When summer was over, he would be the head treasurer at the Phoenix, an off-Broadway theatre.

He loved show business, he told me, and would do anything it took to keep working in it. But his big desire was to produce. "One day," he told me, and the way he said it I knew without a doubt it would happen, "I will make my way to Hollywood and produce movies."

Concerning my dilemma, he suggested we put our heads together and think up a solution. I remember sitting with him in his tiny box office that night after the show was over and cutting the stamps off all two-hundred envelopes. Then we readdressed the new envelopes and glued the cut stamps onto them, this time on the correct side. We worked until four o'clock in the morning, and then went out in his rented white Plymouth Valiant to the local diner, where we had coffee and pancakes drenched in maple syrup, and listened to Jack Jones singing "Call Me Irresponsible" for five cents a play. They were mopping the floor with some ammonia-smelling stuff when we finally left.

I got a few hours of sleep in the room I rented several blocks from the theatre, but he didn't have time to drive home to his apartment in New York City and get back in time to work, so that night he slept in his car. When he woke up, he showered and shaved in the custodian's rooms located behind the giant tent. No one had ever put themselves out so much for me before and it kind of scared me.

After that, he began buying lunch for the two of us, sandwiches from a deli near his apartment. Every few days we would sit on the wooden green bench near the tent, share our brown bag lunch together and talk.

I told him how much I loved the Neighborhood Playhouse. It was a relief to talk about myself as an aspiring actress and not about the other self that was a Main Line debutante. There was a freedom in not being the self that grew up with a menagerie of wild animals that everyone always wanted to ask questions about. It was liberating not being the daughter of adventurers who traveled the world for half a year at a time, the writers of books. To him, I was just who he saw. An ordinary nineteen-year-old girl who was starting her life and desperately wanted to be an actress.

He brought in short scenes from plays that we read together on the bench after lunch. We did scenes from *The Glass Menagerie* by Tennessee Williams and *Splendor in the Grass* by William Inge. At first it felt peculiar, too personal, too intimate, sitting on a bench with a man in a suit and tie, exchanging lines from profound plays. But after a few weeks, I began to loosen up and feel less out of my depth. Was it because I felt no judgment from him? I was like a child who, having learned to walk, was now learning to run and skip and prance and even do cartwheels.

He told me about his life growing up in Manhattan and then the Bronx. Before his mother Beatrice had married his father, she had been an associate to Audrey Wood, the legendary theatrical and literary agent who represented not only the likes of Tennessee Williams, Carson McCullers, William Inge, those same playwrights we had been reading, but Robert Anderson, Studs Terkel and Arthur Kopit, as well. His father, Peter von Zerneck, was born in Austria-Hungary and had come to the United States on the arm of the actress Gloria Swanson during the 1939 New York World's Fair.

Beatrice had come to America as an infant, carried through Ellis Island by her parents, who were Sephardic Jews emigrating from Turkey. She was petite, always dressed in fashionable suits, stockings and high heels, and smart as a whip. Peter was a handsome man, tall, slim, with long, thick blond hair (that had to be held down with a hairnet at night, I was told, or else it went wild). Peter's first agent in New York was Audrey Wood and so it was through Miss Wood that Beatrice and Peter first met, fell in love, and married. Frank was born soon after that.

Beatrice and Peter had three sons, and because Beatrice had given up her position at the agency, Peter was the sole provider. He had worked in half a dozen Broadway and off-Broadway plays, in live television and was a featured actor in most of Alfred Hitchcock's movies. He also worked for Voice of America, since he could speak five different languages: French, Russian, German, Italian and, of course, English. They lived on Holland Avenue in the Bronx, in a one-bedroom apartment where Frank's bed was actually a cot hidden behind the couch in the living room. His mother was an extremely neat person; therefore, all his toys had to be small enough to be kept under the cot, totally out of sight. The joke of the family, he told me, was if you got up in the middle of the night to go to the bathroom, your bed would be made before you got back.

I loved hearing about his family. It reminded me so much of my time at Aunt Aimee's, everyone living so close together. No one seemed lonely.

Nineteen

STATE MENTAL HOSPITAL

———————

There were so many people in the room, I could barely breathe. Water trickled down my legs.

I glanced down at Mafia Whore's big black stomping shoes. They were quiet now. She brushed her unwashed hair away from her face, and for the first time since I had met her seven months ago, I saw her small bear-like eyes flash with tenderness. Not only were they bright, but they were intensely focused. My heart gave a jolt. "You better get her the fuck out of here," she told one of the nurses. "She's only got a few hours before her sacred Second Coming arrives."

"Now we will both have babies," Theresa whispered in my ear, as she held her own baby doll close.

> During contractions, the abdomen becomes hard. Between contractions, the uterus relaxes and the abdomen becomes soft. Contractions move in a wave-like motion from the top of the uterus to the bottom. Labor dries up the fluid in the baby's lungs, which, until now, had been helping them to mature. The lungs now prepare to expand and fill with air.

Twenty

WHAT A DIFFERENCE A DAY MAKES

My job every night, the week that *Finian's Rainbow* played at the Westbury Music Fair, was to stand at the top of aisle eight with a jar of cold cream and two large washcloths. (This was a theatre in the round, with eight descending aisles that led to a round stage in the center below.) When an actor, his face and hands covered in black make-up, ran up the aisle, I was to quickly dab on the cold cream and rub the black make-up off so he could run back down the aisle thirty seconds later, returning to the stage as a white man.

On opening night, I was at the top of the aisle ten minutes a-head of time. Just as we had rehearsed several times that day, the moment the actor in black-face reached me, I quickly slapped the cold cream onto his face and hands and hurriedly began to wipe. But nothing happened. I scrubbed harder. Still nothing.

"It just ain't gonna come off," a bass baritone voice whispered in my ear. "You're on the wrong aisle, kid. You want that man," he said, pointing diagonally across the heads of hundreds of audience members to the man with the painted face, standing at the top of another aisle looking around impatiently... for me.

That night Frank took me to the Tivoli, the local bar where everything was covered completely in red leather, and where the live band's closing song every night, six nights a week was "Shangri-La". Over several very stiff drinks, he explained to me that what had happened that evening was not the end of the world like I thought it was. It was the end of a very hard moment in time, which I would grow to realize some day soon. It was also just one of a thousand hard moments I would have in my life.

Sliding his hand across the table toward mine, and gently fitting his fingers in between mine as though completing a puzzle, he told me I would not only survive tonight but I would also triumph over it. Because of tonight, he said, and because of other times like it yet to come, I would grow mighty and strong. Anything I believed possible, he told me, our hands wound together now, would be possible. I was the kind of person who would always be growing. Growth begets change. Change is imperative to your essence, your spirit, and your core.

As he talked, I began to sense the beginnings of a self-belief I didn't think I'd ever experience. Was it his words or the touch of his fingers?

That was the night I was comforted and reassured.

That was the night I knew it was possible for me to be courageous.

That was the night I first knew I was in love.

That was the night I lost my virginity.

And that was the night I most likely conceived my first-born.

What a difference a day makes—twenty-four little hours.

***

After that we couldn't keep away from one another. Several weeks later, he invited me to stay with him overnight at his apartment in New York City. The box office opened up late on Sunday mornings and Jim Hay kindly gave me the morning off. So I drove with him late on Saturday night, to his apartment on East

91st Street. On the car ride down we held hands. Just the touch of him and the scent of his Old Spice cologne sent a shudder up and down my body.

We drove through the late night and reached Manhattan. He knew the city like the back of his warm hand. Nothing disturbed him as he wove in and out of traffic. When he found a parking place on his street, he was ecstatic. "This never happens," he told me as he jumped out of the car and raced around in his gentlemanly fashion and opened my door. The building he lived in was six stories high. I'd never been in an apartment building in New York City before. The moment we entered I could hear and smell the accumulation of everyone who was living there. I could hear voices from behind locked doors, screaming from an upper floor, coughing from another floor and some laughing, too. Although it was well past midnight, a boy of about eight came out from one of the doors across the way and begged a cigarette for his mother.

When we went into his apartment, when the door with the triple locks was closed behind us and relocked again, our world suddenly turned silent. It was just the two of us standing in the dark. I could hear his breathing. There was nothing left to say between us. He turned and pressed me against the door and kissed me hard. He kissed me again and again and made love to me right there and then, right against his front door, its wood panels pressing into my back. Then we moved from the door and into the living room, no more than four steps away. He showed me his yellow pullout couch. He didn't pull the couch out to make it into a bed, however. We didn't have the time or the inclination for that. Instead, we made love again on the wall-to-wall carpeted floor in front of the couch. Next to the living room was the kitchen. We made love again, there, on the white linoleum floor. We made love in the walk-through closet filled with pinstriped suits, oxford shirts and an array of ties. The last room of the apartment was the bathroom. We made love in there, too. After that, we slept a deep, long, satisfied sleep.

I was the first up the next morning and I had no trouble finding my way to the bathroom. It was straight ahead. Everything was straight ahead because it was a railroad apartment. One room led to another, to another, to another, just like railway cars.

Suddenly, there was a knock on the door. I threw on my raincoat.

"Can I help you?" I called out, wondering if I shouldn't wake Frank.

"Do you have a cigarette for my mother?" a boy's voice called out through the door. When I unlocked it, I saw it was the same boy from the night before. I looked at him and shook my head 'no'. He was so very thin. And his hair could have used a combing.

"What's your name?" I asked.

"Ralphy," he answered.

"Hi, Ralphy," I said.

"Do you have any money?" he wanted to know.

I reached into my raincoat pockets. I had five dollars and some change.

"I can get my mother a pack of cigarettes and you some coffee, if you want."

I gave him my five dollars. "Get me two coffees, will you please?" I called after him. "And I'll give the cigarettes to your mother myself."

"Oh, that's okay," he yelled over his shoulder, before disappearing out the door of the building. "She's at work. I'll give them to her when she gets home."

I followed him out and stood on the stoop. The street was teeming with people. Kids roller skating, men washing their cars, women gathered in their church dresses, talking and rocking babies on their hips. I was amazed at how many people could occupy a single block. *Could I live in a place like this? Yes,* I thought, *I could. In fact, I would love it.*

Ralphy came back with two paper cups. I took them from him and went back inside. Frank, a big bold smile on his face, greeted me at the door. His grin was so wide and he seemed so pleased to see me. He took the cups from my hands, set them down, and kissed me deeply. Then he kissed me again and led me into the living room. The couch was still pulled out from the night before. We fell onto it.

***

It was a little after noon that Monday when a beautiful woman burst through the door of the office I worked in at the Westbury Theatre. "Where is my husband!" she demanded angrily.

"Your husband?" I inquired earnestly. She was gorgeous. She looked like Marilyn Monroe, blonde and very voluptuous. She had on a black linen suit and was wearing black high heels. She looked at me, turned, and stormed out of the office. She slammed the door so hard it bounced back open again. When I heard her ask someone where the box office was, I froze in my chair.

"They are separated," Jim Hay told me.

He had pulled a chair close to mine and was staring at me very seriously.

"She had moved out," he went on. "They've been separated a while. Then he met you."

I looked up at him. "But they are still married," I said.

Jim nodded.

"Why didn't he tell me? Why didn't you?"

"It wasn't my place. But someone saw you. When you were at his apartment. A kid saw you. The kid told her when she went there to get some things early this morning. Then she drove right up here. They're talking now. You may want to go back to your room. She's pretty hot under the collar right now. Come on, I'll drive you over there until this all settles down."

I picked up my purse and followed Jim out of the office and toward his car. I looked to the box office and I could see the woman and him, in his pinstriped suit, walking in the direction of our green bench under the willow tree. I turned away and squeezed my eyes closed.

***

Late that afternoon, I was asleep on my bed when I heard a knock. It had to be him—he had come to explain everything. I got up, rushed to the door and opened it. But it wasn't him. It was my mother, my father and my grandmother, Rose Junker.

"We are here to take you home," my father said. I didn't look at him. I didn't look at my mother. I kissed my grandmother's cheek and she gave me a hug. I was numb. How had they known to come and get me? Who had called them? Had he? Had Jim? I felt dead. I packed up my things without a word from anyone and carried my suitcase out the door, down the steps, to the car. I didn't say a word because my grandmother was there. I knew that that was why they had brought her, to silence me, to silence us all. How could we speak about the unspeakable?

My father drove the car onto the Staten Island Ferry. When the boat began to move he got out of the car. "Come on, I've never been on this ferry before. Let's explore." I got out and followed him to the back of the boat. I leaned on the railing next to my father, as we both watched New York disappear into the past.

"I love him. I really do."

"You'll get over it."

"I don't think so."

"We'll see."

"He's Jewish, you know."

"Let's keep that between us. Don't tell your mother."

I nodded and looked out at foam churning up behind the ferry. What was happening? What had just happened? Was it all over? Just like that?

***

"She's pregnant," the family gynecologist told my mother a week later. Why he didn't tell me first, I'll never know.

Twenty-One

STATE MENTAL HOSPITAL

I looked out the car window as I was driven away. I saw all their faces looking out at me through the thick mesh windows on the fourth floor; Mafia Whore, Theresa, The DuPont Executive's Wife, some of the Zombies and a few of the nurses. Would I see them again? I didn't know. I still didn't know anything. My heart lunged in my chest. We passed the recreation cage and I could see a huge purple heart drawn on the dark asphalt. Shooting out from around it, like a first-grader's painting, were chalk lines of sunny yellow. *Oh, Theresa,* I thought.

Just as the car passed through the hospital gates I felt the first cramp. I took in a deep breath and let it out slowly. A few minutes later another cramp seized me, only this time I let out a moan.

"Better hurry," the nurse next to me called up to the driver. "It's starting."

As we picked up speed I felt another contraction. This one was even more severe than the last and I let out a scream.

> When regular contractions begin, your baby moves down into the pelvis as the cervix both effaces and dilates. She will twist and turn during labor to find the easiest way to squeeze through. You may feel strong contractions that last 30-60 seconds and come every 5 to 20 minutes. Your contractions will gradually become stronger, last longer and be more painful.

Twenty-Two

EXPECTING

My mother called me into the living room at Sunny Hill Farm and asked me to sit down. My father was nowhere to be seen.

"You are pregnant," she said. "The doctor told me you are two months along."

I stared up at her as if she were speaking a foreign language, one that I hadn't learned yet. Then, slowly, a fear of such magnitude filled me that I was forced to lean over my knees so that I wouldn't faint. My hands and feet went numb. My mind stopped working. For a moment I didn't exist. I was not in the room. I was not in the world.

Back up in my bedroom, I sat and looked out the window. It was hot. The air was still, even though the window was open. Perspiration gathered on my brow, under my arms, between my breasts and dripped down. The lawn below was brown. The pastures beyond were dried out, too. It had been a hot summer. No rain for months. Just heat, days of long humid heat. I hadn't noticed until now how hot it had been. Not until I'd come back to the farm.

I put my hands on my flat stomach. I felt nothing. What did it mean to be pregnant? It meant being with child. It meant having a baby. It meant... I didn't know what it meant.

An hour later, when I saw my mother get into her car and head down the drive, I went downstairs into her bathroom and took three of her sleeping pills. I had never even taken an aspirin before.

All I wanted to do was sleep. Sleep for a long time. Maybe when I woke up everything would be all right again.

When I woke up five hours later I was in a hospital and my stomach was being pumped.

She tried to kill herself, I heard someone say.

I fell back to sleep and the next time I woke up I was in another hospital, the Psychiatric Institute of Philadelphia. It cost a thousand dollars a day, someone told me later. I assumed that I'd be here for no more than a day or two. Part of me was confused and dazed but another part of me was a little bit thrilled. As a budding actress a chance to be in a mental hospital was extraordinary. To be able to observe crazy people *up close* was a dream for anyone interested in character study. I would be in and out of the hospital in no time with an experience most actresses did not have access to.

The first doctor I met at the Institute of Philadelphia was the one who informed me why I was really there. She had brown curly hair, a severely pockmarked face, and warm dark eyes that could see into the center of you.

"Do you know why you are here?" she asked me.

I shook my head 'no'.

"Your parents and the admitting doctor," she stopped to look down at the papers stacked up on her desk, "—who I see here is also your gynecologist," she looked back up at me, "which is very unusual—" she continued to watch me as she went on, "all feel you are suicidal."

I looked at her, confused.

"Are you suicidal?" she asked.

I shook my head 'no'.

"It says here that you took an overdose of sleeping medication and had to be taken to the hospital to have your stomach pumped."

"I took three of my mother's sleeping pills. I wanted to sleep," I told her. "I wanted to sleep for a long time, but I didn't want to kill myself."

Crossing her arms, she placed them firmly on her desk and leaned forward.

"Your parents want you to get an abortion," she told me. "As you know, abortions are illegal in this country. But there is such a thing as a therapeutic abortion. If the mother is in any danger during her pregnancy, medically or mentally, then a medical doctor is permitted to perform an abortion."

She sat back.

"Do you want an abortion?" she asked.

I felt a storm of rage fill me up, hot lava pouring through my veins. No one had mentioned anything about an abortion to me.

She slid a legal paper across the desk for me to sign.

"If you do want an abortion, please sign here. It will not be performed without your permission. It's your choice. "

My mother was trying to get me declared suicidal so I could get a therapeutic abortion? I was stunned. The breath had been knocked out of me. There were no words that could express how betrayed I felt. There was just a deep profound wound in the center of my heart.

I did not take the pen offered to me. I did not sign the bottom of the document. Not because I was a Catholic, not because I was against abortion. I did not sign the document because it was my choice not to sign it. My choice was to give birth to my child. It was the very first real, burning choice that I had ever had to make and I made it without any regret.

I stood. I turned. I left the office. I had been in a mental hospital for several days. Now I was ready to go home.

***

But I was not taken home. Instead, I was kept at that first-class sanatorium for a month, and when my parents' insurance ran out I was transferred to the state hospital, still under the guise of being a suicidal patient.

That silence became my state of being there is how, I think, I saved myself. In the end, I found that refusing to talk had given me a sense of control where I had none before. I found great power behind my unspoken words. I found a sense of peace, too.

***

I spent hours in my room at the state hospital imagining what my baby would be like; a happy little child, with long blonde hair like mine, and beautiful brown eyes like her father's (eyes that I would never forget, eyes that I would remember for the rest of my life). I imagined her laugh. I imagined her small hands. I imagined her running and jumping and rolling down hills. Little by little, I began to think of what I wanted for my daughter when she was born: a mother, a father, a home, a room of her own and a happy, *ordinary* life. And that's when I understood—I couldn't give her any of these things. Someone else would have to.

***

The Catholic Charities Hospital in Philadelphia was stark, flooded in florescent light. Two nuns wearing white wheeled me on a stretcher, put me in a hallway next to a fourteen-year-old girl who was having twins, and we both screamed in agony together.

Several hours later, on April 19, 1964, I gave birth to a beautiful and healthy baby girl. I named her Aimee Veronica. Aimee after my aunt, and Veronica after Saint Veronica, who was the one to give Jesus her veil to wipe his forehead with, on his way to being crucified.

The name Aimee means *love*. The name Veronica means *bearer of victory*.

I was allowed to see her only once, from five feet away, before I gave her up for adoption.

"Hi there," I called to her. "I love you very much."

She turned her head and seemed to hear me.

Then someone took me by the arm and led me out of the room.

Outside, I fell into a nearby chair and cried and cried and cried.

> Many mothers are surprised to see how alert their newborn is. Right after birth, a newborn's eyes can be open much of the time. Some babies are able to study their mothers' faces. Your baby may turn or react to the sound of your voice.

Daniel Pratt Mannix, IV,
swallowing a sword, circa 1940

MIDDLE: Little Julie in the
incubator at Bryn Mawr Hospital,
Pennsylvania.
May, 1943

BOTTOM: Julie in playpen with pet
skunk. 1944

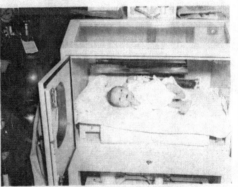

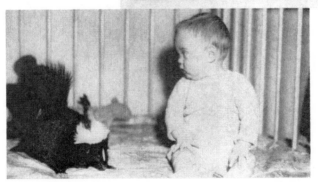

LEFT: Julie, age 6, with governess. First
Holy Communion, Isle of Capri

RIGHT: Peter and Beatrice von Zerneck, Frank's parents, circa 1940

Jule and Dan Mannix with Rani the cheetah and Aguila the eagle in Malibu,
California, circa 1950

Julie, age 7, with Rani in Malibu, California

Jupo helping herself in the shed icebox

Age 17, with Macho

Mannix family with Rani the cheetah, in the 'big living room' at Sunny Hill Farm

Julie with John Cromwell, 'Corky' Wheat, Poppy Mull, and red-plumed llamas in the circus ring at her debutante party. Sunny Hill Farm, June 1962

PART II

Kathy

Twenty-Three

AIMEE MEETS HER FAMILY

"She's a screamer," the nuns at the hospital for unwed mothers warned as they handed me to my parents. "We think she just needs some attention."

The Sisters of Charity were right; I was born with an insatiable desire to be noticed and wasn't afraid to show my unlikable side if it meant all eyes would be on me. My grandfather called it a mean streak, my father deemed it determination, my mother, who had waited ten long years for me, simply smiled.

My life story does not begin in that downtown Philadelphia hospital, however. It begins fifteen years earlier with a priest holding a flashlight, a young man named Frank Wisler, and an eighteen-year-old blue-eyed brunette.

Frank noticed her the second she walked into the Holy Cross social. She was tall and elegant and possessed a charm powerful enough to render every other female invisible. Within ten minutes he knew her name, Kathy Conway, and after the knock of those four syllables he knew his life would never be the same. Holy Cross held "spot dances" occasionally; a priest would mingle among the dancers and turn a flashlight on a couple nearby. Each of the dancers got five bucks. Frank and Kathy won ten that night.

Three years later, in 1952, Kathy Conway surrendered her surname and became the feminine half of a union to be known as Mr. and Mrs. Frank Wisler. Within a few years they owned a home in the suburbs, drove a new car, and enjoyed a wide circle of family and friends. Things seemed to be falling into place for this engineer and legal secretary. Except for one thing: children.

In February of 1962, my parents adopted their first child, a mild-mannered, blue-eyed baby boy whom they named Frank after our father. Two years later they returned to Catholic Charities for me, a rosy-cheeked, brown-eyed brunette with a smidge of an attitude. They named me Kathleen after my mother.

I'll never forget the day my younger brother Jerry joined our family after we moved to Florida in 1966. I woke from my after-noon nap, climbed over my bed rail, and set off to find my mother, who was usually in the family room, reading a book, waiting for me to come snuggle in her lap. I ambled, sleepy-eyed, down the hall-way, and was startled by the sight of a crib set up in the spare bedroom. I tiptoed in to investigate and discovered a sleeping baby tucked underneath a light blue blanket. An unsettling mix of curiosity and irritation roused me, and I poked him until he cried and scurried back to my room to hide under my bed. I heard my mother's footsteps walk toward the room with the crib, where she stood and calmed him and left him to continue his nap. After a few minutes, I returned and studied the infant squatter again before deciding to poke him once more, this time with a vein of jealousy fueling my jab.

Again, I retreated to my hiding spot and waited for my mo-ther's response. Just as before, she returned and spent a few minutes soothing him back to sleep, but instead of returning to the family room, the scuff of her shoes on the terrazzo floor headed down the hallway toward my room. I closed my eyes and when the footsteps stopped, I blinked open to see a pair of penny loafers pointed in my direction at the foot of my bed. I held my breath. Silence. And then she crouched down on her knees, lifted my bed-skirt and said, "I see you've met your brother Jerry."

At the time, it all made perfect sense. This was how babies were born. They simply showed up in a crib one day, most likely via the stork. Pink blanket meant a girl, blue a boy. Yes, it all made perfect sense.

My life as a Wisler had begun seamlessly. I had a big brother to admire, a younger brother to boss around, and doting parents who played with us in the backyard. It was as if I had been dropped into the first chapter of a fairy tale—but we all know how fairy tales go.

Twenty-Four

DEAR MOMMY

My mother was diagnosed with breast cancer in early 1967. I don't remember any talk about her being sick, though the signs were there. Over the course of the next few years, she was in and out of the hospital for weeks at a time. While Dad was at work, my grandparents would take us to visit her in the hospital. Children were not allowed on the cancer wing, so the nurses would wheel my mother to her third floor window. From the grassy area below, my two brothers and I would show off our finger paintings and perform perfectly executed cartwheels for her to admire. These hospital visits became a normal part of our routine, like a trip to the grocery store or a Saturday matinee.

Toward the end, my grandparents took on all the responsibilities of running our home. Mom spent most of her time sleeping, but when she was awake she'd call for my brothers and me by ringing a small brass bell she kept on her nightstand. We would race to her room and sit hip to hip on my father's side of the bed where we strained to hear her fantastic tales of angels floating down from their castles atop the white, puffy clouds, to live, undetected, among us, helping with homework and dinner dishes.

"If you close your eyes and sit very still," she would whisper with her eyes pinched shut, "you can feel your own guardian angel."

The thought of invisible angels frightened Jerry, who was now three, prompting him to curl up under our mother's frail arms, where she would stroke his thick brown hair and reassure him. "Don't be afraid, my dear little Jerry, your guardian angel *protects* you."

"Don't worry, Jerry," I would interrupt in an attempt to recapture some of my mother's attention, "my angel's friends with your angel."

Although her voice was small and her breathing shallow, she always found the strength for story time each afternoon.

The last month of her life, Mom dropped to a fleshless sixty-five pounds and spent all of her time in bed or wrapped in a blanket on the family room couch. I sat outside her bathroom door each morning and listened to the running bath water and the strange accent of the homebound nurse, Ingeborg, as she cared for my mother. Hospitals, nurses, and her emaciated body: the evidence was there. I should have been frightened. I should have been sad. I was almost six, Frankie was nine; we were old enough to put it together. But our parents were decidedly protective and managed to make suspect circumstances seem completely normal.

It was my mother's nature to be cheerful and unfailingly positive. Dad said even her oncologist, a close family friend, was flabbergasted by her sunny outlook, warning that, "one day she is going to wake up and realize she is dying." Until the very end, however, my mother stayed true to her optimistic disposition.

Mom passed away in May of 1970. My brothers and I each mourned her in different ways: my older brother was controlled and pragmatic, speaking about her in measured doses; my younger brother was undone; and I wrote her letters, placing them in a shoebox under my bed, hoping I would one day find them replaced by her handwritten replies.

May, 1971

Dear Mommy,

Jerry cries for you every night, but I told him when he's seven like me he won't cry anymore.

Love, Kathleen

***

I believe a mother is one of the most influential persons in a child's life. She breathes life into her child's character with her choice of words, displays of tenderness, and her daily example. Although I only had six years with my mother, her impact on me was immeasurable.

I wonder if she realized how carefully I observed her patience the day someone cut in front of us at the grocery store checkout, or if she knew I was listening the afternoon she told the man on the phone she wasn't able to subscribe to the newspaper he was offering, but that he had been the most courteous salesman to ever call. Could she have known that each of those insignificant, ordinary moments taught me more about who I wanted to be than anything else she did? It is for that reason that I treasure the run-of-the-mill recollections of my mother the most.

I only have a handful of memories of her, but they are rich and well-rooted. These mental impressions fit comfortably into a thirty-second loop that repeatedly runs on the Family Channel in my mind. My most distinct memory takes me back to a sunny spring Florida afternoon. My father's mother, Mom-Mom, visiting from Philadelphia, was peeling potatoes on an open page of newspaper at the kitchen table. I loved to sit at this particular table. Besides being the epicenter of our home, it provided the best view of my favorite backyard tree, a thirty-five-foot Australian pine. As a climber of all things taller than me, that pine was my Mount Everest and there wasn't a day that went by that I didn't attempt to climb its strapping limbs.

I was engrossed in my own thoughts when suddenly I heard the front door open. Trance broken, I looked down the narrow hallway to see my mother's coiffed silhouette in the square of the doorframe. She had just returned from her monthly visit to the beauty parlor. I ran to her, nearly knocking her over as she gracefully stepped into the foyer. She bent down to hug me, her purse falling forward down her arm, meeting the small of my back. She wore a soft pink, belted dress with a Peter Pan collar and smelled of scented hairspray and the outside world. At that moment, her "Mommy" aura was absent—she looked like one of those pictures in the ladies' magazines.

"Mommy, can I feel it?" I begged.

She smiled and tipped her head forward. I carefully investigated her black swooping bangs, neatly organized above her bright blue eyes.

"Wow! How do they do that?" I asked.

"It's hairspray," she answered. "One day I'll take you with me."

To this day, the smell of Aquanet takes me back to that moment.

Twenty-Five

PHILADELPHIA SUMMERS

Within weeks of my mother's passing, my paternal grandparents moved into our den, which had been Dad's office. This wood-paneled sanctum was the one room to which I was not ever granted free access. Its doors were always closed, as if to keep in its intoxicating scent—a woody bouquet of cedar, sage, and jasmine that possessed an undeniable restorative quality. It was the perfect room for Mom-Mom and Pop-Pop, as they would certainly need a steady supply of vigor to care for three active children who had just lost their mother.

Rather than enduring that first summer with us alone in Florida, it was decided my grandparents would take my brothers and me to the Philadelphia suburbs, where twenty-five first cousins and a myriad of adoring aunts and uncles awaited us. My mother's side of the family, the Conways, was also well represented there, and over the years had established a sound friendship with the Wisler side. In fact, I was unaware that there were *two sides* of a family until I was much older.

Frankie, Jerry and I were given room and board and enough love to fill an ocean at Aunt Jean's house. Aunt Jean, Uncle Jack, and their seven kids lived in Bucks County on a winding, tree-lined street that was neatly peppered with spacious two-story homes occupied by neighborly people who didn't find it an imposition to smile and wave at a child happening by.

There was never a shortage of fun at Aunt Jean's. Each day

seemed to possess its own magical charm. One day we might spend hours upon hours perfecting our belly flops and cannonballs off the diving board; another day, we might decide to transform the basement into a haunted mansion and spend the day spinning cobwebs out of yarn and dressing up like vampires and witches.

The highlight of the summer was the two weeks we spent together down at the Jersey shore. Each of my four aunts' families rented homes within blocks of one another. Dad also flew up from Florida to join us for a week. Each evening, Dad and my uncles were relegated to the task of taking the lively group of us twenty-eight cousins for a stroll along the boardwalk or to the local ice cream shop.

On the last evening of our Jersey shore excursion, our fathers would kick the night off with a sunset viewing over the bay followed by the long-anticipated trip to the local amusement park, where we would eat cotton candy and ride roller coasters until we threw up.

Like clockwork, upon my return to Aunt Jean's from our days at the shore, I would experience a siege of swimmer's ear. This ailment would strike mercilessly at about 2 a.m., feeling like an explosion of lava running through my ear canal. I remember the first summer I experienced it.

I slept with my cousin Suzanne, the fifth child of seven and the middle daughter.

"Suzanne, wake up," I whimpered as I untangled myself from the grip of her legs. "My ear," I said, tears springing from the corners of my eyes, "it really hurts."

Pain shot through my nerves with each word I uttered.

"I'll get my mom," she whispered as she slid out of bed and disappeared down the dark hallway.

Moments later Aunt Jean appeared, clad in her cotton night-gown, her short blonde curls pressed unevenly against the side of her head. Despite her petite frame, she easily lifted me from the bed and carried me out of the room.

"Let's find some oil, kiddo," she said, as if we were embarking on some type of adventure.

Like Dad, Aunt Jean always had a pleasant expression on her face—and I could feel this in the cadence of her speech. She found the oil, warmed it by running hot tap water over it, and dispensed a few drops into my ear. Navigating the shadowy hallway like a seasoned sea captain, she carried me to the well-worn Windsor rocking chair and held me as if I were her own child, pulling me close to her chest, quieting my sobs with soft hushes and hums.

I could feel her breath on my face. I buried myself in her embrace and imagined I was in the arms of my own mother, feeling her fingers stroke my hair, hearing her voice sing to me. I closed my eyes and allowed myself a moment of vulnerability—a moment to miss *her*—a moment to fall apart while in the safety of *her* arms.

***

Soon, July turned into August, the grimmest month of my year, the month I had to say goodbye to my dandelion-yellow utopia: a world filled with the welcome distractions from a life without my mother.

The two-day drive back to Florida with Mom-Mom and Pop-

Pop was therapeutic. My brothers and I were dejected and hopeless in Pennsylvania, Maryland, and Virginia; however, those feelings started to abate in the Carolinas. By Georgia, we were back to the business of picking fights with one another one minute and giggling uncontrollably the next. At the end of our journey, Dad was always there to greet us in the driveway, no matter the time of day or day of the week. His *welcome home* embrace signaled the end of summer and the beginning of a new school year.

Twenty-Six

FORK IN THE ROAD

It didn't take long to settle into a new routine—a routine governed by my grandmother and enforced by my father and grandfather. On school days, my brothers and I had breakfast together. As we ate, Mom-Mom, clad in a floral housecoat and slippers, sat on a stool adjacent to the kitchen table and answered our off-the-cuff questions.

"Mom-Mom," I would ask, "why is milk white?"

Without pause, she would begin a detailed explanation. "Milk gets its coloring from a protein called casein. The whiter the milk, the more fattening it is." She would quickly expand the topic to include cow trivia. "Did you know most cows produce 90 glasses of milk per day?"

Mom-Mom had an 8th grade education, yet could speak more intelligently on any topic than most college graduates. Some days I learned more at the breakfast table than I did during my seven hours of school.

After school, we were greeted with a snack; then we changed from our school uniforms into our play clothes, which were always laid out on our bed, and joined the neighborhood kids in a game of street ball or hide 'n' seek or tag. Our daily routine was predictable and uncluttered and just what we needed to feel secure.

By the time Dad arrived home from work each evening, we were tousled with evidence of the day's fun. After a mandatory up-to-the-elbow hand washing, we gathered in the dining room for a homemade dinner, usually something German and something that had been stewing, simmering, or slow-baking all day.

Dad and Pop-Pop sat at opposite ends of the very long, wooden table with Mom-Mom and me on one side and my brothers, Frankie and Jerry, on the other. Dinner was the one meal during the day we shared with our father, and Dad seemed to make the most of it. He would start lively conversations about our day, forging through our initial answers of "good" and "nothing" to the questions, "How was your day?" and "What did you learn in school?"

After the dinner dishes were washed, dried, and put away, my brothers and I tackled our homework. Dad and Pop-Pop sat at the dining room table with us while we dotted our *i*'s, crossed our *t*'s, and solved for *x*.

Math was my Achilles heel, but Dad would tirelessly work problems with me until I understood concepts. This was no easy task, since the subject easily frustrated me. I was quick to cry and scribble angrily all over my paper if a problem presented a challenge. But Dad was a natural teacher, possessing the patience of Job and an encyclopedic intellect.

During my angry outbursts his voice would take on an austere but composed tone. "Kathleen, pull out a new sheet of paper. Let's solve this problem step by step." He guided me well, recognizing the value of example and the futility of lecture.

Dad, like my mother, always made time for my brothers and me. Despite the demands of his job as an electrical engineer, he somehow found the time to take us on camping trips, to throw the ball with us in the backyard, and to teach us how to fix a flat bicycle tire. He was a dad who was completely present—physically as well as emotionally. Every car ride, every meal together, every kiss goodnight was an opportunity for a meaningful conversation with his kids. He was the heart of our home.

In spite of the structure, in spite of the devotion, in spite of all the nurturing, I had trouble adjusting to life without my mother and found reasons to rebel. I was, after all, the middle child and according to psychologists, I had a fifty-fifty chance of being the peacemaker or the renegade.

According to Sister Rose Bernadette, my second grade teacher, I had become the renegade, earning a far less than exemplary 'D minus' on my conduct report. A mandatory parent conference revealed I was "stubborn and ill-tempered" and often sat "cross-armed" with a scowl on my face. It was then that Dad realized I needed an outlet for my pain. A week later, I found myself on the South Beaches softball team, wearing a #10 crimson jersey and matching cap, standing next to second base.

That was the fork in my road: the decision to involve me in organized sports was effective and had a lifelong impact on me. Dad also signed up my brothers for Little League and volunteered to coach Frankie's team. Playing sports in the backyard was part of a normal day for me, but belonging to a team fostered my sense of camaraderie, while satisfying my competitive spirit. I threw all my energy into softball and expelled those irascible demons from my system. And, as if by divine intervention, Sister Rose Bernadette was soon sending letters home singing my praises (which, if you were taught by nuns, you know rarely happens).

Frankie and Kathy, age 1, with parents, Frank and Kathleen Wisler, on the Jersey Shore in 1965

Kathy, age 2, with brother Frankie in
Philadelphia

Kathy, age 4, with mother and
brothers in Indialantic, Florida

Christmas 1968. Kathy, age 4, with
Jerry and Frankie

Kathy, age 4, with brothers. Halloween in Florida, 1968

At Lion Country Safari in West Palm Beach, Florida, age 5

In Philadelphia, age 3

Christmas in Florida, age 7

Twenty-Seven

DAUGHTER SWAP

Over the next three and a half years, my father, brothers, grandparents, and I formed healthy, new branches on our family tree. We had made it through the dry season, and I expected our arrangement would continue on forever, but I would soon learn that change is inevitable.

I first noticed something was different at dinner one evening. Dad was twitching his fingers, the telltale sign that he was upset. My grandfather, usually alive with stories about feeding marshmallows to the golf course alligators, sat in silence. Instead of the normal laughter and conversation, the only sound I heard was chewing and the continuous patter of metal forks on porcelain dishes. The silence was deafening, and, after a few minutes, it was simply too much for me to bear.

"Mom-Mom?" I asked. "Why are carrots orange?"

"That's it!" my grandfather pounded both fists on the table. "Frank, we're done!"

"I didn't choose this," Dad bellowed back. Realizing his audience, he pulled back and said, "Please, let's talk about this later."

After dinner, Dad and my grandfather went for a drive and returned in good spirits. I got the feeling that both needed to vent and now that they had, things would go back to normal. I was wrong.

The following weekend we met Gloria.

Gloria Douglas-McCoy had caught my dad's eye at church. She was a tall, slender, blue-eyed redhead with a luminous smile and spontaneous laugh. Although she was only a few years younger than my dad, her forty years seemed much less than my Dad's forty-five, and I was drawn to her youthful energy. I remember the first night I met her. She sat in our family room with both feet up on the hassock, smartly dressed in a well-cut jacket over apple-green bell bottoms and cork platforms, engrossed in easy conversation, eating a slice of my grandmother's key lime pie. Dad had an undeniable glow in his eyes that night—a look I hadn't seen since my mother.

"She reminds me of Mom," I said approvingly, the very next day.

The following Sunday, after 12:15 Mass, I found myself going home with Gloria; just me—alone, without my brothers. As my grandmother handed me a bag of play clothes, she explained that Dad and Gloria thought it would be a good idea to swap daughters for a few hours.

"Swap daughters?" I sharply replied. "Gloria has daughters?"

"Yes," I was told. "She has twins."

Gloria's twins were nine, one year younger than I was, and although we attended the same small Catholic school, I had never heard of them.

Dad introduced us in the church parking lot. "Kathleen, this is Tracey and this is Melissa. Tracey and Melissa, Kathleen."

Gloria's daughters were fraternal twins. Melissa, lanky and frail, shyly said 'hello' and quickly turned away, jerking the mousy brown braid that ran the length of her back over her shoulder.

Tracey had a ruggedness about her that immediately told me she was the dominant of the two. She had an unkempt appearance—long and unruly strawberry-blonde locks, a round face flecked with freckles and the scars of a recent bout of chicken pox, tobacco-colored eyes, and a thick waistline accentuated by the splitting seams of her homemade dress. They were not at all what I would have imagined the daughters of the polished Gloria would look like.

Tracey and I smiled nervously at one another before heading off in opposite directions.

Gloria, fashionably dressed in a turquoise wrap-dress and matching shoes, grabbed my hand and whisked me off to her car, where an elderly woman was waiting quietly in the backseat.

"Hi," I said as I got in next to her. "I'm Kathleen."

"I'm Honey," the old woman sweetly said as she inched over to make room for me. Honey was Gloria's grandmother, a widow in her early eighties who seemed naturally kind and especially good with children. Like Gloria, she had a sprightliness that drew me in.

It only took a few minutes to drive to Gloria's house, which was really Honey's house, where we sat down for a lunch of corned beef, cabbage, boiled red potatoes, and sweet tea. Despite the shock of learning of the twins, I felt at home with Gloria and Honey and soon realized they felt the same about my family and me.

"They broke the mold after they made your father," Gloria cooed. "I've never met such a generous man."

"And you, Kathleen, are just like your father—a real sweetheart," Honey quickly added.

After lunch, I helped Honey with the dishes as Gloria excused herself and went upstairs. When the last plate was washed and dried and put away, Honey and I sat on the back porch and played a couple of games of tic-tac-toe with sidewalk chalk. After letting me win more than my share of games, she suggested I spend the rest of the afternoon exploring the backyard tree fort.

"The twins fixed it up like a princess's castle," Honey explained. "If these old legs could climb, I'd join you. Go on and have fun!"

Excitedly, I stood up, clapped the chalk off my hands, and headed off. But before I could make it down the porch steps, Gloria swung open the screen door behind me and said, "Where do you think you're going?"

I turned around; there stood Gloria—barefoot, clad in an old pair of cut-off jeans and a stained undershirt, her long, red hair haphazardly pulled back in a ponytail. One hand was holding back the screen door she just slammed open, and the other hand held a cigarette and a pint-sized mason jar filled with iced tea.

"Get back in here, young lady," she growled. "At our house we do chores before we go out to play."

Embarrassment flooded my face, turning it a scarlet red. I looked over at Honey and then back at Gloria, hoping to see a hint of a smile on one of their faces.

"Start with the newspapers," Gloria said, placing emphasis on the word *start*.

That *I'm just kidding* smile never came, and, for the next hour, I gathered renegade sections of Sunday's paper, made beds and fluffed pillows, and dusted a wall of white bookcases in the living room. I labored in silence, partly because I didn't know what to say, but mostly because I was afraid. Really afraid. My silence, however, was simply a window dressing for the disturbed beehive vibrating loudly in my mind, which buzzed recklessly from one thought to another. *What did I do? She was so nice. I don't like her. I'm never coming back. Just wait 'til I tell Dad.*

After my chores were completed, I sat alone in the living room on a gray tweed couch facing the wall of bookshelves. Quietly, I scanned the room for clues to unravel the reason behind Gloria's bizarre behavior. I focused on the bookshelves; besides a few books on hairstyles and Girl Scout badges, there was a parade of old figurines interrupted by a decorative picture frame containing a photo of Gloria wearing a baby-blue uniform and a pillbox hat. I pitched forward to get a better look.

"Isn't she beautiful?" Honey softly said. I hadn't noticed her stretched out in the recliner behind the couch.

I turned around, startled, but Honey's soft smile put me at ease.

"That's when she worked for Pan American," she said proudly. "After leaving her second husband, she decided to become a stewardess."

"Second husband," I blurted out without thinking.

"Yes," Honey grinned. "Though the twins are from her third husband. She quit the airlines after they were born."

That day I saw another layer of Gloria—the layer clearly displayed under the glass of a fancy picture frame, the layer with three ex-husbands, twin daughters, and an unpredictable temperament. By the day's end, I didn't care to see any more.

Without warning, the well-dressed, polished Gloria emerged from her bedroom sporting a white Charlie's Angels pant suit and smelling like a capful of White Shoulders.

"Kath-a-leen-a," she chirped as she swung her loosely curled, bright auburn mane over her shoulder. "We've had a big day. Let's do this again!"

I wanted to roll my eyes and tell her I'd rather work math problems all day. I wanted to run home and tell Dad that I was wrong, that Gloria was nothing like my mom, but I smiled instead and choked out a polite, "I can't wait."

The stench of my afternoon dissipated with every minute we traveled toward my home. Not surprisingly, in that short time I compartmentalized the events of my unsettling day. After my mother's death, I had become adept at creating an island for problems, keeping them a comfortable distance away from my daily life and visiting them later, after I'd had time to sort them out. By the time we rolled up my driveway, I had sent this experience to a remote haven called 'Won't Do That Again.'

"Did you have a good time?" Dad asked me as Gloria and I walked through the front door.

"Yes," I lied. "It was fun."

Later that evening, Frankie asked the same question.

"She's mean," I replied.

Twenty-Eight

THE MERGE

We saw a lot of Gloria and her daughters over the next few months. They joined us for dinner, accompanied us to the movies, and became a regular presence in our lives. The "Barefoot Gloria" had vanished as quickly as she had appeared; frankly, I was starting to wonder if I had overreacted that day. If Dad, the smartest man I knew, trusted her, then I should too, I reasoned. It wasn't long before I dropped my guard and warmed up to her again.

After a short courtship, Dad married Gloria. Everyone was on their best behavior for the first six months after the merge. Although my brothers and I missed our own mother, we knew she wasn't coming back. She was gone. And despite Dad's best efforts, we needed the influence of a woman in our lives just as much as the twins needed a reliable father figure in theirs. It was clear from the start that we all wanted this new family to work.

The adjustment period wasn't easy, however. Sharing a room for the first time was difficult for me. I bristled at having to sacrifice space for the benefit of not one, but two other girls. Tracey's messiness had not been obvious to me until I became her stepsister. Before the day she put her roots down in my room, I hadn't noticed that she was a knick-knack hoarder who also rescued second-hand stuffed animals. Within days of moving into my room, it was obvious by the one-eyed teddy bears and assorted puppy dogs and kitty cats lined up against each of the four walls, that she, too, had never had to share a bedroom.

Fortunately, Melissa's baggage was minimal. She collected *Planet of the Apes* action figures and kept them neatly stored in a very large bread box covered with Wacky Pack stickers. She, unlike her sister, seemed to appreciate orderliness and routine. This became apparent on Saturday mornings when she would lay the apes out on her bed and wipe their rubbery heads with a wet washcloth before packing them up and sliding them back beneath her bed.

Although having new sisters was, at first, uncomfortable for me, I soon realized that I didn't mind sharing my room with them, after all. Melissa was quiet and, it turned out, mostly kept to herself and, fortunately, Tracey, albeit unconcerned with boundaries, was good at taking hints. After I'd gathered her herd of animals off the floor several times and piled them in a heap in the closet, I was glad to see the day when she finally confined them to her bed, never again to venture any further.

A few weeks after the wedding, Gloria began to suggest that Dad adopt the twins. *Wouldn't it be nice if all the children had the same last name?* she buzzed daily. Dad soon agreed and, in the interest of becoming a united family, he legally adopted the twins. Tracey and Melissa's biological father, who hadn't seen them since he had remarried and moved 2,500 miles away to Oregon, seemed especially happy about this decision and allowed the adoption to go through at lightning speed.

Soon after the adoption was finalized, the mood of our home began to change. It was as if Gloria woke up one morning, and realizing her probationary period was over, began to shed her girdle of pretense.

The change, however, happened intermittently. At first it could only be detected by me, the one who had witnessed the "Barefoot Gloria" a year prior. A change in her appearance was the signal for her change in mood. On the days she sported the just-rolled-out-of-bed look, she was short-tempered. The rare days she donned lipstick and shoes would prove to be her best days—days where she would help with homework, laugh at jokes, and delight in making a delicious, home-cooked meal.

It seemed the honeymoon was over. "Just stay out of her way," my older brother Frankie suggested. He understood my need to be noticed and urged me to "go for a bike ride" each time he saw me getting on Gloria's nerves.

Soon, the bad days started to outnumber the good. I say *days* because her irritable moods were reserved for the days my dad was at work. When Dad walked through the door each evening, she morphed into June Cleaver. One minute she'd be scolding us, "Finish your homework, you miserable brats!" and the next minute, upon hearing Dad's car pull into the garage, she'd singsong her finish ten octaves higher, "You hear me, little darlings?" It was creepy.

At first, Gloria's abrasive treatment was purely verbal, but she was soon doling out smacks, and when that didn't satisfy her, beatings became the norm.

Such was the day one rainy afternoon when my younger brother Jerry, a second-grader at the time, crawled up on Gloria's lap to watch an episode of *Gilligan's Island*. I watched from the corner of my eye as she tenderly held him in her arms and stroked his thick, brown hair. After a minute, he changed positions and elbowed Gloria in the ribs. Her knee-jerk reaction was to shove him off and wildly smack his head.

"That hurt!" she hollered as she continued to hit him.

My knee-jerk reaction was to protect my little brother.

"He didn't mean it!" I jumped up, holding my hands up in the air like a police officer directing oncoming traffic to stop.

Gloria paused, stood, and taking a minute to catch her breath, looked down at me. I hadn't realized how tall she was until that moment.

"And who do you think you are?" she said, giving each word its own moment. "I am the mother in this house, young lady," she continued. "Go to your room!" And, as if to punctuate her final statement, she drew back her hand and delivered a sharp, stinging blow to my backside.

This was the first time she hit me—it was the test smack, the experimental swat, an inch of the yardstick by which all future licks would be measured. I soon learned from the intensity of later punishments that questioning authority on behalf of my brother was a misdemeanor offense, at best. Referring to her in third person, "She said I could..." warranted a Dial soap mouth-washing. Rolling my eyes during her "I do so much for you" speeches earned me a ponytail yank that would put nine out of ten people in a neck brace.

PART III

Julie

Twenty-Nine

A GHOST

I did not realize that I wouldn't be returning to EPPI when they drove me away after giving birth. I did not realize that I would be going back to Sunny Hill Farm. I certainly did not realize it would hurt this much to leave my baby at the Catholic Charities Hospital. I ached for her... I grieved for her... I kept seeing her tiny face, her little head covered with a soft cap of brown hair; her large dark eyes filled with excitement for her new life—a life I would never be a part of. I cried and cried. It felt like I would never stop.

There were other things, too. I had been living away from Sunny Hill Farm now for almost two years. I wasn't used to living where everyone around me had to walk on eggshells. The patients in the hospitals had been candid, straightforward, and yes, dangerous. Maybe crazy out of their minds, but they were always honest. When I entered a room now, conversations stopped, eyes were raised in hopes of judging how I was feeling at that moment, and then counterfeit smiles would shine up at me. Neither my baby nor my stays at the psychiatric institutes were ever mentioned. In fact, as expected, there were many words left unsaid. My parents and I avoided eye contact—I could not look at them, and they would not look at me. So I stayed in my room. I missed Mafia Whore standing guard over me—and I especially missed Theresa. However, it was clearly apparent that I wasn't crazy, after all. They had released me after the baby's birth, hadn't they.

And then there was Frank. The last time I had spoken to him was the day before I was taken to the Psychiatric Institute of Philadelphia, right before I took the sleeping pills. I had reached him in the box office at the Westbury Music Fair.

"It's me. Can you talk?"

"Of course I can talk. I've been trying to reach you."

"Why didn't you tell me you were married?"

"I didn't tell you because I thought I would lose you. I knew you wouldn't want to go out with a married man."

"I'm pregnant."

Silence.

"I have to go now. I don't think we should talk again."

"Please. I love you. I am getting a divorce. I know we can figure this..."

I hung up the phone. I loved him but I knew I couldn't trust him. I didn't believe a word he said. I never wanted to see or talk to him again.

***

My second week home I began to venture out of my room, but only late at night when everyone was asleep. I felt like a ghost in my white cotton nightgown as I floated from room to room. One night I came across my mother sitting in the dark of the living room. We both gasped. I could smell the bourbon she was drinking. I turned around immediately and went back upstairs and did not come down again for the rest of the week.

My third week home I decided I couldn't go on like this anymore. Rising before dawn, I dressed in my old baggy gym clothes, the only clothes that fit, and went out for a run. The morning dew dampened my socks and sneakers, and it felt good to have the wind against my face after all these months. I just kept running. I walked and ran, walked and ran all day and thought about what I was going to do with the rest of my life.

Thirty

THRESHOLD OF LIFE

A month after I returned home, I was preparing for my first outing. The one and only dress in my closet that actually came close to almost fitting me was a royal blue linen sundress, but it was cut too low and showed too much. I threw a white sweater with pearl buttons over my shoulders.

I was very hesitant about being out in the world again and having anyone see me. I had told my mother that I wasn't ready to go out yet. It had only been four weeks. "It'll do you good to see some friends. You can't stay cooped up here forever," she had answered. I doubted that very strongly, but even I knew I couldn't, as my mother had put it, stay cooped up at Sunny Hill Farm forever.

As I dressed, I began to contemplate. My mother was a logical woman. But, I thought further, she was remarkably illogical, too. She was very skilled at justifying her moral decision-making. The perfect example of this being her willingness for me, despite the fact that she considered herself a devout Catholic, to have an abortion. Her justification for this? Her daughter was suicidal—which, of course, I wasn't. I suspect she truly did believe, however, that she was saving my life. As I had saved the life of my baby—*deep breath... watch out... don't think about the baby... danger coming... beware*—my mother must have believed that she had saved mine.

It hit me unexpectedly, rapidly, like a whip, one where the slash marks make their impressions deep and bloody. I slid to the floor in front of the mirror where I was standing and held myself in my arms. The ache for my baby began again. But I knew how to cope with it now. Gradually, I began to make myself go cold, thoughtless and without feeling. "I don't care, I don't care, I can't care," I repeated over and over again, trying to gain access to that part of me that was without sensation. "She is better off where she is. With a family—a mother and a father. Living a safe, ordinary life."

***

There were about twenty people at the party, which was held out in the garden. I knew everyone there, at least casually.

"You've been gone a while," someone I had gone out with a few times, never really liked and now began to despise, told me as he offered me a gin and tonic several minutes after I arrived. His hair was combed as if his mother had done it for him and he was wearing an energetic madras jacket.

"Well, Africa… how was it?" he asked smugly. "You were traveling in Africa these last months, weren't you?"

So that is what my mother had told everyone. That I had been traveling in Africa. It was, however, something she had neglected to tell me.

I took a sip of my drink and nodded.

"Well, Africa certainly seems to have suited you," he went on, smiling like the fox that he was.

I smiled back, trying to look indifferent as I sipped again at my gin and tonic. In a minute, I would walk away. I just had to have somewhere to walk to. I looked around for a friendly face.

"Your breasts are much larger now," he suddenly said very nonchalantly, freezing me in my place. He continued, his smile widening. "In fact, they really are quite voluptuous."

I was immobilized. No one had ever talked to me like this before. I didn't know what to do.

He took another sip and then continued on like a cat playing with a mouse. "Your breasts have delicate little veins in them, too. Why do you think that is?"

What does he know? I wondered in a panic. Did he know everything? Did he know about the hospitals, the baby? Did *everyone* know everything? My mother had sent me into the lion's den and I was totally unprepared, unarmed.

"I hear you have been awfully naughty. You left us a child and returned to us a woman," he proclaimed. He was really enjoying himself.

Suddenly I felt a fury take over my body. *How dare he*, I thought. No matter what had happened to me, he had no right to talk to me like this. I reached out and slapped him across the face. "Fuck you, McDonnell," I said, in true Mafia Whore form.

It gave me great joy to see Brian McDonnell's tanned face turn a pasty white. He stared at me for a brief moment and then, without a word, he walked away and headed to the bar.

Good old Brian McDonnell had been right about one thing. I had indeed left the Main Line as a child and returned from somewhere else as a woman. And very soon now, with the help of my mother—who had no idea she was assisting me to this end—I would move away forever.

Thirty-One

ACTING DAYS

My mother was very good at organizing things. She was able to arrange for a not-quite-six-year-old daughter to board at several different Sacred Heart Academies around the world when it was against their policy to do so. She was also very good at getting a pregnant daughter into mental hospitals.

Luckily, my mother, with all her determination, was also first-rate at getting her daughter a position as an apprentice at one of the most highly thought of summer theatres in the country. The Bucks County Playhouse in Pennsylvania was close enough to New York City for every agent, casting director and producer to be able to drive there easily any summer afternoon or evening.

From that June to early September, Bucks County Playhouse became my life and I loved every grueling moment of it. With seven other apprentices, I worked at the theatre in temperatures as high as 110 degrees, under blasting sun and drenching rain, from seven in the morning until seven at night, building sets, painting flats, sewing costumes, collecting props, setting up lighting and refinishing furniture. Then, from 7:30 p.m. until midnight, we ushered people to their seats and sold programs, candy and drinks, after which we raced backstage to help actors in and out of costumes; we assisted with the lighting and sound, and changed the sets in between scenes. When the show was over and the audience and actors were gone, we cleaned everything up, discarding cups and programs, finally sweeping the stage at the very end. And, if we were lucky—incredibly, extraordinarily lucky—some of us were actually given small parts in the plays, which meant studying lines, and rehearsing, along with all the other work we were required to do.

But however much I loved my time at the Playhouse, I had to go off by myself so I could feel my grief without alarming others. *She* was almost two months old when I arrived there. Had I been able to keep her, maybe I would be listening to the sound of her first laugh now, breathing in her scent, feeling the grasp of her fingers.

I also began seeing Frank again in New Hope, Pennsylvania, quite an appropriate name for a town where I was to begin my life anew. The weeks I had been at Sunny Hill Farm, the only telephone left connected had been the one in my parents' bedroom, and off limits to me. Breaking a promise I had made to my mother, shortly after she dropped me off at the Bucks County Playhouse, I called him from a phone booth next door. He was at the Phoenix Theatre in New York City.

"I called to let you know that I had the baby. She was a girl. I gave her up for adoption. I thought you had a right to know."

"Oh my God. I can't believe this. Are you okay?"

"I'm alright."

"Can I see you?"

"No."

"I'm divorced now."

Silence.

"I called your house to let you know. I left messages. I called every week. Mostly, they hung up on me but once in a while I got a word in."

Silence.

"I really want to see you. Even if it's just once. Just so we can talk."

"Okay. I'll see you once. And that's all."

He drove to New Hope the following Saturday in a rented car, arriving around midnight. We met at a coffee house and talked about the baby. I told him I named her Aimee and that she had brown eyes like his. He reached out and took my hand. Tears welled up in his eyes. A wave of love filled me suddenly. I tore my hand away. I stood up. "Alright," I said. "We've met. Now it's time for you to go." "I can't," he said. "I can't leave you now that I finally have you again."

He came back the next day, and during my lunch break we sat by the waterfall near the theatre and shared a sandwich. We talked about how it felt giving Aimee up for adoption and wondered what it would have been like to keep her. He returned a few days later, despite the fact that I had asked him not to. We talked some more. He told me he wished he had done things differently. "I was certain," he said, "that if you knew I was married you would have nothing to do with me. But I *really* was separated. I *really* was getting a divorce. Please forgive me. Let me make it up to you. Please give me another chance." When I saw how distraught he was, I began to believe him.

"If only—" I started, but tears stopped me. He held me as I cried, rocking me. "If only," I managed to go on, "I'd known you were waiting for me all this time. If only I'd known there was a chance. If only I had known there was a possibility. We would be a family now. If only..."

He was the first and only person with whom I could share my pain. It was such a relief to be able to talk to someone who cared as much as I did. Slowly, I began to feel connected to him again. Slowly, I began to trust him.

For the rest of my stay at the Playhouse, he visited me every Sunday night and stayed through Monday.

***

Lionel Larner was one of the most excellent gentlemen General Artists Corporation, the famed agency, had ever engaged. He was a renowned agent, exceptionally handsome, very English, and incredibly dapper; he always wore a three-piece suit. Every week, Mr. Larner made a habit of driving his green Jaguar from New York City to the Bucks County Playhouse to see the new plays. It was during one of these plays, starring the comedian Shelley Berman, that Mr. Larner witnessed the debut of a very young and extremely inexperienced apprentice actress as she strode across the stage and bungled her one and only line so unintelligibly that the audience became hysterical with laughter. The line that I bungled had to do with the word 'philanthropist'.

Of course, I was thoroughly humiliated and cried myself to sleep that night, despite being assured that I had not made a fool of myself because the audience had all thought it had been part of the play. Several days later, a postcard arrived at the Playhouse and it was addressed to me. The card was engraved with GENERAL ARTISTS CORPORATION at the top and was from Mr. Lionel Larner. It was an invitation to visit him at his agency in New York City to talk about representing me as an actress.

"He is one of the most important talent agents in New York," Frank said over the phone.

When I called my mother to tell her about the postcard, she phoned Mr. Larner immediately to make an appointment for me. The day after the season was over at the Bucks County Playhouse, my mother and I took a train to New York City where she had booked a room for us at the Gotham Hotel just off Fifth Avenue. Never let it be said she let any grass grow under her feet if there was an opportunity to be seized.

Thirty-Two

AND THEN...

I dreamt that everything was going to be all right. When I woke up it was morning and the wind was blasting. *Rise up on this glorious day and be the best you can be,* I said to myself.

My mother had bought me a blue linen dress at Best & Co. —to match my eyes, she said—along with black heels, a pocket book and a pair of gloves. I was so thin from all my work at the theatre I was barely a size two. She had brought with her the pearls my grandmother had given me for my sixteenth birthday. I was very tan from being outside working all summer. I had no make-up on except for a touch of lipstick and my hair was white-blonde from the sun.

Just before leaving the hotel my mother whispered, "Bless yourself, Julie."

And, of course, I did. I crossed myself twice.

My mother was a real wheeler-dealer in Lionel Larner's office at General Artists Corporation that late morning. She was at the top of her game.

We were served coffee as we sat in our ritzy leather chairs across from Mr. Larner's elegant and empty desk. He looked nail-bitingly imposing except for the enjoyable fact that his eyes were totally focused on me. *And he was smiling.* He said he truly enjoyed my performance. *He was smiling.* He said I actually lit up the stage. *He was smiling.* He said he was thrilled I responded to his letter.

He asked me about my acting training. I told him about my year at the Neighborhood Playhouse. I told him about my summer at The Bucks County Summer Theatre. I was afraid I might be stuttering. I was terrified that I was talking too much, which I could do when I got on a jag. I was petrified I might not be talking at all and just thought I was.

"Why didn't you go back for your second year at the Neighborhood Playhouse?" he asked.

This was not a question I expected. I was not prepared. The air in the room stopped flowing. My mouth went dry as a bone.

"She was traveling," my mother stepped in seamlessly.

With great effort I captured my breath again.

"I was traveling," I repeated.

I was certain my face was aglow with perspiration.

"I was traveling around Europe. It was amazing. I will never forget it."

"Oh, how fantastic," Mr. Larner said. "Tell me, where in Europe?" He seemed genuinely interested.

"Well, I was in France for a while," I told him.

"She was stag hunting with the Count de Vergie and his family on their estate," my mother added. "She lived with the family in their château for several months."

"Yes, they keep truffle pigs in their moat, which is dry now. I was in England, too, in Devon, hunting with the Devon and Somerset Staghounds."

"She lived with friends of ours, a veterinarian and his wife, helping out. We have wild animals, you know. That's what we do."

My mother and I went back and forth like a tag team, replacing my recent history with summer travel stories from my distant past.

"My father is a writer. We have a menagerie about which he writes books."

"My husband writes about other things, too; the history of torture, the Hellfire Club, gladiators. Historical subjects that interest him. He uses pictures of Julie in a lot of his magazine articles. She's been in *Life* and *Collier's* and over two-dozen other magazines. She's been in front of a camera since the day she was born."

This give-and-take between my mother and me was like us rallying around a flagpole; my mother and I flying together into the light, my mother and I leaping from the top of a ferocious waterfall, hand in hand, eyes closed, screaming. It had never happened before, this *mother and I* thing. Now that I'd had my first taste I was ravenous for more. I didn't want it to be over. If only time could stand still. If only the past could disappear.

Lionel Larner leaned forward in his chair totally caught up in the thrill of the ride we had invited him on. He wanted more. His eyes begged us for more.

But then, abruptly, the ride was over.

Fifteen minutes after the meeting had begun, my mother pulled up the sleeve of her linen jacket and looked at her watch. I stared at her. What was she doing? Our train back to Philadelphia didn't leave until late that afternoon. We were in no hurry. Besides, wasn't this my meeting, my interview? I had a sudden impulse to grab her arm and tear the watch off. I steadied myself.

"Is everything all right, Mrs. Mannix? This is the correct time of our appointment, isn't it?" Lionel Larner asked in his very polite English accent.

"I am so sorry," my mother said, looking up very contrite. "We are going to have to go in a few minutes. I am afraid that I have made Julie's next appointment sooner than I should have. Please forgive me. I am not accustomed to situations like this."

"No, of course," Lionel Larner said gallantly, rising from behind his desk. "Of course you aren't. Where is your next appointment? Perhaps I can get someone to help you with a taxi."

"The William Morris Agency," she told him.

"The William Morris Agency..." Lionel Larner repeated. This smart-looking Englishman didn't know with whom he was dealing. But I did.

Within half an hour I was signed with General Artists Corporation, one of the top agencies in the world, with offices in New York, London, Paris and Los Angeles.

My mother and I left the building feeling full of ourselves, gleeful with success. As we walked downtown to Penn Station, an August breeze whipped around the corner of Madison Avenue. Along with it came a girl my age wearing a sundress. She was pushing a baby carriage. When she passed by us, a gust lifted the flowered skirt of her dress and waved it at me like a flapping flag. The baby inside the carriage was wearing a little pink dress with a matching hat. Her large blue eyes caught mine. A spasm of pain wrenched my body. My heart skipped a beat. I began to tremble. *Oh God, oh God, help me. What have I done?* I was falling. I leaned back against a red brick building to steady myself. I stretched out my arms so that the palms of my hands, my fingertips, could feel the rough *brickness* of it, the violence of it. *Oh God, oh God, help me.* I dug into the bricks with my fingernails.

"Julie, are you all right?" my mother asked.

I stared at her.

She took my hand and looked into the palm like she was a fortune-teller. It was wounded, the skin broken.

"You can't do this now," she said. "Not now. Not when everything is going so well."

She took out her white handkerchief and cleaned my hand.

And this was how they would come, my unexpected depressions. And this was the way it was. And this was the way it would be, it seemed, forever.

Thirty-Three

A NEW LIFE

On a beautiful morning in mid-September, my mother left me off at the Paoli station, where I bought a one-way ticket for the early train to New York City. It was the train business folk took, the ones dressed in suits and ties, dresses and high heels, carrying leather briefcases. I was carrying two suitcases with my initials, J.H.M., stamped under the handle. I stepped onto the train and turned to wave to my mother.

The train came to a slow, sliding, screeching halt as it arrived at Penn Station. I carried my suitcases to a taxi and gave the driver an address. I had one hundred dollars in my black purse to last me the month. The room at the Hotel for Women on Lexington Avenue, which I would be sharing with two other girls, had been paid for in advance. It was small and crammed full. It took me ten minutes to unpack. I looked at my watch. It was close to noon.

He still lived in the railroad apartment on East 91st. The sun was high, shining brightly, and the brownstones along the street glowed. The air smelled rich with the change of seasons. I could hear singing coming from my heart. I had called him the day before from a phone booth outside the Paoli Newsstand. "Tomorrow," I had whispered, "I'm coming tomorrow."

I knocked on his door and he opened it. We didn't touch. We didn't kiss. We didn't hurry. We stared at each other.

I noticed the pullout bed in his living room was made up neatly into a couch. The yellow wall-to-wall carpet under it had vacuum marks. The white linoleum kitchen floor was still damp from being mopped. But when he took me in his arms and kissed me, the room around me faded away and I went limp, and liquefied.

***

The scent of coffee brewing woke me up an hour later. "I'm going to shave. Then maybe we can go for a walk in Central Park," he told me, handing me a mug of coffee. "Then we'll go to the theatre," he said. "You'll love Rosemary Harris and Ellis Rabb. Everyone in the back office knows about you. You're all I talk about."

We walked down to the Phoenix Theatre. Halfway there, it started to rain. I looked like a drowned rat when we arrived.

"This is the girl I love," he told everyone he introduced me to backstage.

"This is the girl I love," he told everyone in the front offices.

"This is the girl I love," he told me and kissed my nose.

***

What were the odds of my getting a job in New York City two weeks later, as an actress/model for a magazine called *Modern Romance*? What were the odds that my mother would actually spot my picture a month later on the cover of the magazine, with the words, "I Was Forced to Have My Mama's Sin Child" printed boldly underneath?

She called me at the only number she had, which was the

phone outside the small cluttered room at the Hotel for Women. I had stayed there only three nights so far. She had caught me there only because I was picking up some clothes.

"Julie, after everything that's happened, how could you do such a thing? I am so embarrassed for you. It's not even a flattering picture. You look like a tramp, a little whore." Her voice was like a plate of glass, smooth, even, dangerously level and on the verge of shattering.

"The magazine pays fifty dollars a session. That's just the first of many, Mother." I neglected to tell her I had gotten the job with Frank's help, who was friendly with the photographer.

"What about your acting? You are there to act!"

"It *is* acting, Mother. *Modern Romance* only uses actors. It was my first acting job."

"Does Lionel Larner know about this?"

"No."

She hung up without another word.

My first real acting job was for a Sunday morning religious show, "Look Up And Live". I got the part by auditioning for Robert Dale Martin, a casting director who was also a friend of Frank's. Then I got another job for Avon make-up and then a three-page layout in a teen magazine called *Scholastic*. Yet, I still hadn't made more than two hundred dollars. I couldn't be totally dependent on Frank, so I found a part-time job as a hostess during the lunch rush at the Madison Deli on the corner of 86th Street and Madison Avenue. Both the customers and the waiters ate me alive there, but every day I got free pastrami sandwiches, thick ones even a large mouth couldn't wrap around. They oozed smells that made my mouth water. Wrapping them in foil every afternoon, I brought them back to 91st Street, where we shared them for dinner on the small white table in the kitchen. My black leather purse smelled of pastrami for the rest of its limited life.

Fellow theatre manager Oscar Olson saw my picture on Frank's desk. His wife was a well-known casting director. She was looking to cast the understudy to the female lead in a forthcoming Broadway play, *Poor Richard* by Jean Kerr, starring Alan Bates, Gene Hackman and Joanna Pettet, that was to open at the Helen Hayes Theatre. I auditioned once, twice, three times on a huge empty stage. I was a speck dressed in my tailored tweed suit. Next to me sat my black purse, smelling of pastrami. The director, Peter Wood, was English. He bounded on stage after my last audition and shook my hand.

"Lovely, Miss Mannix," he told me. "The job is yours."

I was silly with pleasure when I walked off the dark stage on wobbly knees and headed into the brilliant light of 46th Street. *The job is yours.* Had he actually said that? I was crazy with joy, high as a kite. *The job is yours.* I couldn't believe it. It was too much for my soul to bear. I had to stop and jump up and down in place, so I looked like a nutcase dancing, hopping, skipping, prancing along Broadway as I headed up and over to 91st Street so I could share my incredible news with Frank. I would tell him they said *the job is yours.* He would be so, so proud. Less than a year ago I had been locked away in a state hospital for the criminally insane. Just eight months ago I had given birth to my baby. Soon after that I had given her up for adoption. And now I was here, on Broadway, and days away from starting rehearsals.

"Just an understudy," was my mother's response when I called to tell her my news that evening.

"An understudy for a lead part in a Broadway play, Mother," I explained. "If the lead actress gets sick, I will go on in her place."

"Will you be home for Thanksgiving? It's at the end of the month."

"The play goes on the road for tryouts and I'll be going with them. I'll be in New Haven and then Boston for Thanksgiving, Mother. They rehearse the understudies every day."

"This can't be very good for your career, Julie. Does Mr. Larner know about this?"

"Yes, Mother. He drew up the contract. I am getting paid a lot of money. He's very proud of me."

"Oh," she said. "That's good."

"Mom..." I hesitated and then, with my heart in my mouth, I went on. "I'm going to come home tomorrow. I have something I need to tell you."

I borrowed his rented car, a white Dodge Dart, and drove out of New York City, through New Jersey, and then onto the Pennsylvania Turnpike. Two hours later, I was driving up Route 401 and then winding my way up the quarter mile drive of Sunny Hill Farm.

"Whose car is that?" my mother asked.

"It's his," I told her.

She stared into my face. The clock in the kitchen on the old Formica table ticked away. She just kept looking at me. *Tick tock, tick tock, tick tock* went the clock. *Beat, beat* went my heart. The house was silent. My brother was away at school. My father was probably in his room writing. She just kept looking at me. Her face was blank. Expressionless. We were the same size. Our faces were the same shape, we had the same nose. People had always said how much we looked alike. I didn't think so. She was much prettier.

She continued to stare, then abruptly turned and walked away. I would never again see her the way she had been.

My father came out into the kitchen in his wrinkled brown cord pants and worn wool plaid shirt.

"Don't ever try to get in touch with us again," he told me. He turned and went out. I hadn't expected this—for my father to turn his back on me and walk away...

The clock in the kitchen stopped ticking. It did that sometimes. For no reason at all it would stop ticking for a few minutes and then start up again. I think it must have lost time and every so often someone reset it. When I turned to leave, the clock was still silent. The kitchen was soundless. The only sound that could be heard was the sound of my heart banging like a bongo in my torso. My chest clenched, released, clenched, released, trying to squeeze all the hurt out. But there had been so much of it—too much, too much loss. I had not had enough time to heal. How could I heal if I didn't have enough time between wounds? Everything was happening so fast. I had no time to catch up.

***

My body throbbed for my daughter daily. Whenever I heard the sounds of a baby, my body became alert: *is it her? It could be her. I could take her and run.* And I was brought to my knees, sobbing and choking.

This melancholy would come over me suddenly, when I least

expected it. This melancholy came as a huge dark wave and covered me over in hopelessness, drowned me in despair. This was an injurious, wretched melancholy, stones-in-pockets-and-walking-into-the-lake kind of melancholy. It was a *beast*. A bloodthirsty beast that wanted me gutted so it could feast upon my innards.

I missed Mafia Whore and Theresa and especially the comforting padded cell where I could beat and cry against the wall. That's what New York City needs: soundproof, padded cells that you can rent by the hour.

Thirty-Four

THE VOW

I had never dreamed of having a large white wedding surrounded by family and friends. It seemed indecent, such an invasion of such a private moment. On an ice-cold morning in January 1965, Julie Hawthorne Mannix and Francis Ernest von Zerneck were pronounced husband and wife in front of the Justice of the Peace in Westbury, Long Island, just a couple of miles from the Music Fair tent where they met. I wore a lovely cobalt blue wool suit I'd found hanging on a rack in a second-hand store on Eighth Avenue; the suit was ten dollars and a pair of brown leather gloves that matched my heels, even less. Frank wore his pinstriped suit and looked breathtakingly handsome with his thick dark hair all slicked back.

"I choose you as the person with whom I will spend my life," he said.

"I choose you as the person with whom I will spend my life," I agreed.

From then on, whenever I was down for the count, "indisposed", comatose, he sang to me. He sang with his arms outstretched like he was Frank Sinatra himself. *Women do get weary,* he crooned, *and when she's weary, try a little tenderness.* He knew the lyrics to all the songs from Broadway musicals and when he forgot the words, he'd fill in with whistling.

There were bells on the hill,
But I never heard them ringing,
No, I never heard them at all,
Till there was you.

There were birds in the sky
But I never saw them winging,
No, I never saw them at all,
Till there was you.

Sometimes he got down on his knees and looked up at me. *Only you, you are my destiny. Only you and you alone,* he sang out.

Sometimes it worked, and sometimes he just had to sit with me in silence until my melancholy passed and we could both breathe again.

***

Lionel Larner sent me up for feature films, television shows and a lot of commercials. I was soon cast as the Maxwell House wife. For an entire half-year I could be assured of turning on the television any time of the day or night and see myself, very close up, sipping at a steaming cup of Maxwell House coffee and smiling brightly. Then I was cast in a half dozen other national commercials as well as several soap operas on which I had reoccurring roles. My face was everywhere on television. So much was happening to me. I could hardly keep up. Who was I now? I was a wife, I was an actress, and I was one of a million in a crowd pouring into Central Park to try and cool off from the broiling New York City heat that summer.

Thirty-Five

A STROKE

Then, very early one morning, while my mother was walking out to the pasture with a bucket of feed for the Bantam chickens, she suddenly keeled over. And that was it. Her whole life was changed in the time it took the sun to splatter a path of light from the shed door of Sunny Hill Farm to the barn, one hundred feet away. No one had expected this turn of events, especially not my father.

Although my parents had totally erased me from their lives—I had been disinherited, disowned, cut out of the will—I was tracked down and I got a call within hours.

"Come home, Julie," my father begged me over the phone. I hadn't heard his voice in over a year. He began to sob. "Your mother needs you."

"I'm coming," I told him. "I'll be there tomorrow morning." I was starring in a play at the Olney Theatre north of Washington, D.C. Luckily, the next day was the one day in the week the show wasn't playing. Everything that had happened between my parents and me before this phone call was suddenly set aside, put on hold.

I was also three months pregnant, but not showing at all. I decided not to mention it to either of my parents. Not for the moment, anyway.

My mother was never the same after her stroke. She tried but she just never was. She learned to talk again after much therapy; she learned to walk again, but with braces on both of her legs. She did very little smiling for a very long time. I think she was in a lot of pain, but she never complained. She was so accustomed to being able to do what she wanted when she wanted, that without that freedom, her essence just seemed to evaporate. Worst of all for her, though, was the fact that she needed help to do every little thing.

Meanwhile, my father was like a boy in a man's body, incapable of functioning in this new world. He couldn't even write. Instead, he went for long walks in the woods with an eagle on his wrist.

When I reached my sixth month it became visibly obvious that I was pregnant. Understandably, though, they were too overwhelmed with their own situation to notice.

I thought my mother had gone stark crazy when she called me one day and told me that she had finally found the perfect person to come and live at Sunny Hill Farm and help her out. "She... is very... un... unusual," she announced haltingly but proudly. "I feel she is... is the best... best person that I have... interviewed... (long pause)... and she... she is here now. Father and I... we just... picked... her up. Her name is... Margret. She... doesn't speak... English. Only... German."

"That is really terrific," I said when my mother had finished. I wanted to know more, but I didn't want to ask her to talk any longer. I knew she was exhausted. I could barely understand the last few words she had spoken.

"I'll take the train home tomorrow, Mom, so I can meet her. I can't wait. Congratulations."

My belly was bulging now and I was wearing wide dresses when I was with my parents to conceal the fact. *Poor Julie,* I imagined them thinking if they noticed at all, *she's getting quite fat*. It was Margret who was the first to remark on the fact that I was heavy with child. She was a big woman and her face was without expression. She wore men's black shoes. On our first meeting, she gently laid her large hands on my stomach and smiled. "Baby," she said. I loved her at first sight. She reminded me of a gentler Mafia Whore.

Margret. Well, I'll begin with where my mother found Margret and that was in the Phoenixville Mental Hospital. No one knew why she had been there. She looked to be in her mid-sixties and was a hundred pounds overweight. Her hair, what there was of it, was white, and her skin tone was white too, ghost white, never-seen-the-light-of-day white. She also rocked. She rocked back and forth from the day I met her, till the day I last saw her, fifteen years later. As my mother had said, Margret spoke German only, although she did have a half a dozen words of English that she threw in here and there, the word *baby*, happily, being one of them. She was afraid of no one and nothing. On her second day at Sunny Hill Farm, Margret helped my father carry all fifteen feet of Peter the python into the guest bathtub so he could finally have a proper bath after all those months. Margret could muck out a horse's stall in no time, kill six rats and feed them to six falcons and then bring the falcons in for the night, without flinching.

Margret could also cook a mean lamb stew, biscuits from scratch, dozens of chocolate chip cookies and still have the energy to carry my mother out into the garden twice daily, once in the morning and once in the afternoon, so my mother could get back the lovely suntan she so very much wanted.

It was through Margret's eyes that my parents finally saw me.

"Baby. Good baby," she said and patted my belly every time I visited.

"When are you expecting?" my father finally asked late one afternoon, as I struggled into his car at the Paoli train station.

"In three weeks. The end of December," I told him.

"Your mother and I are happy for you."

"Thank you," I nodded. A tear of gratitude splashed down my cheek.

There was never a single word mentioned about Aimee. It was as if she had never existed.

Thirty-Six

ANOTHER CHANCE

On December 21, 1965, a year and a half after giving away my first child, I gave birth to a glorious little girl. I held her to me and drew in her sweet scent. I inspected and studied each part of her from head to toe. I put my ear on her tiny torso and listened to her heartbeat. She was mine. She was mine to keep. We named her Danielle Frances von Zerneck. What a splendid and dignified name, we thought.

A few days after she was born, it was time to bring her home. I was beyond myself with excitement. I had thought this moment would never come. Proudly, Frank dressed her and finished by wrapping her up in a blanket hand-knit by his mother just for this occasion. The snow was falling silently, softly and thick like cotton balls, covering the ground, as we carried our baby out into the waiting world and took her home.

For the next week, we stayed awake every night listening to her breathing. Her bassinet was at the foot of our bed. We took turns getting up to check on her in case she had tossed off her blanket. For reasons that are mysterious, she trusted us implicitly.

The first time I took Danielle out in her carriage—this was a carriage given to us by Frank's parents, which of course had to be a huge, shiny, navy blue English pram, as it was for their first grand-child—I pushed it slowly and cautiously out the front door of the new apartment building we now lived in, and then to the corner of

56th Street and Eighth Avenue. It was bitter cold. The sidewalks were icy. She was wearing two sweaters and a pair of mittens, a pink woolen hat and was bundled up in three blankets topped with a handsome navy blue one lined in gray silk, which had been her father's years ago and matched the elegance of the pram. But still, I was certain she was going to freeze to death.

I was headed, for the first time, down to the Martin Beck Theatre, where Frank was the manager, to show my new baby daughter off to everyone there. This ten-block stretch along Eighth Avenue, from 56th Street to 45th, was considered the pimp-center of the Western world, with four prostitutes standing on each corner. Because I'd made this walk twice a day for the past nine months, each of their faces was familiar to me, though we had never been formally introduced. When I reached Eighth Avenue that bitter winter day, I realized, to my absolute horror, that I had no idea how to get the gigantic carriage off the sidewalk and down onto the street. No one had ever taught me how to navigate a pram the size of a small car. Somehow, I had thought that when you became a mother those kinds of things just came to you. Perplexed, I stood there as the arctic wind whipped around me looking to see how other mothers did it. But to my utter dismay I noticed that there were no other baby carriages around. Could there be a law against them in this neighborhood because it was close to Broadway? I didn't know. There was just so much that I didn't know. So, I anxiously tried to figure out how in the world I was going to get my new baby and her illegal carriage, not only over the first curb, but also over the next nineteen, without inadvertently tipping the carriage over and bouncing her out of it. Fear shook my already trembling knees even more. My hormones began to run rampant.

Tears of frustration welled up in my eyes.

I was about to turn around and go back home, when suddenly four guardian angels appeared to save me. They were dressed to the nines in fabulous fake fur maxi coats, with thigh-high leather boots and enough make-up to sink a ship. "Come on, sweetheart," they said. "We'll give you a hand." I knew these women. They had watched me for the last nine months as I got bigger and bigger. I stepped aside. With the seamlessness of athletes, or experienced mothers, they somehow managed to ease the carriage onto its back wheels, off the sidewalk, across the street and then back onto the next curb—without even slightly stirring Danielle. This continued from block to block as we were passed on from one group of Ladies of the Night to the next, each kindly instructing me further in the art of pram-handling, until I finally, by block number ten, had mastered it.

Three months after Danielle's birth, I was cast in a soap opera, *The Doctors*, and soon after that, Frank's parents and their youngest son, Michael, moved into the apartment right below ours so they could care for their granddaughter when we were both working. Beatrice was the kind of mother who bragged about her children and sang their praises, since they were at the very least two cuts above any other child that walked this earth. She had three sons. She never had any doubt that all three would be anything but extremely successful and victorious in all things they attempted. And, it would turn out, she was right.

Beatrice was a strong-minded woman. No namby-pamby there. She got her way with most things. And she taught me so much over the years. She taught me to take the shoelaces out of Danielle's white shoes and then wash and dry them on the radiator. She taught me how to iron the puffed sleeves on her dresses. She taught me that I needed to bring a wet washcloth to Central Park, tucked in a plastic bag, so that after Danielle had finished playing I could clean her up for the ride home in her stroller. She taught me to put Danielle to bed by six so that I would have time for Frank and myself before he would have to go back to the theatre at night. When Danielle danced her fantastic leaping and spinning dances, she shook her grandparents' cut glass Austrian chandelier that hung over the dining room table below. They never once complained.

Six months after I left *The Doctors* I was cast again, as the juvenile lead in another soap opera, *The Secret Storm*, in a part I played for several years. I was accustomed now to rehearsing shouting scenes in the early morning with a cup of coffee in my hand and curlers in my hair. I was used to trying on five or six dresses, pairs of shoes and stacks of jackets and coats at 7:00 a.m., before one was finally chosen. I was not apprehensive when it came to going over lines *out loud,* to myself, as I waited near the set to go on. I was familiar with all three of the cameras pointing at me at once on the set. It didn't make me nervous anymore when the make-up person touched up my lipstick and powdered my forehead as I was going over intimate lines like *I love you, too, darling, and with all my soul,* with my scene partner seconds before the show was to begin. My heart swelled when I heard the words 'quiet on the set' and 'action' and when suddenly everything went silent except for the sound of my voice. I felt the warmth of the lights shining from above and from the sides, and I knew where to turn to say an important line so they would light up my face. I cried on cue and laughed and ranted and raged. And when I forgot a line I knew how to find the cue cards being held off to the side without skipping a beat. At the end of the scene, when the organ, hidden behind a screen, began to play, my breath let itself out and my heart filled with bliss. I was doing it. I had dreamed my world, and now I was living in it.

I loved my role as Wendy Porter. I loved playing a sixteen-year-old girl, though I was then twenty-two. I loved getting up at five-thirty in the morning when it was still dark and walking over to the great brick building that was CBS on West 57th Street, just four blocks from our apartment. Sometimes, when I'd come out in the late afternoon, there were teenaged fans waiting to talk to me. They wanted to know about my hair, about the dress I was wearing the day before, about what Wendy Porter was going to do next to ruin her father and stepmother's marriage. Sometimes I wondered if Mafia Whore or Theresa or The DuPont Executive's Wife watched the show and recognized me.

Always, one of the best parts of my day was coming home to Danielle. She was walking and talking now and scribbling with her crayons on the walls. She had a tent in her room where we would cuddle when I came home, and I would read to her for as long as she would stay still.

But it wasn't all perfect and balanced. Memorizing new lines every day was tough. I had a hard time with that. What took others two hours to do, took me four. And when Frank came home from the theatre at midnight he wanted to talk, but I couldn't. Some days, there were too many drops of water in the glass.

Sometimes, after I left the studio and was walking back home in the late afternoon, I would pass by mothers holding the hands of their preschool-aged children and my heart would drop. It was then that I thought about Aimee the most. In between work and home. When I was all by myself. What was she doing now, I wondered? Where was she? Could she be living in New York City? Could I be walking by her right now and not recognize her? Could I be passing by my own flesh and blood on this very street and not know it? I wondered if today the daughter I had to give away had been sitting on her adoptive mother's lap watching me on television. I tried to remind myself that giving up Aimee had been the best thing for her. She had a family, an ordinary family, something, that at the time, I could not have given her. *But*, I would think again, as I did often, *if I had waited, if only I had waited, maybe I could have kept her. If my parents had been willing to— If Frank had— If only there had been some way.* Some days my heart burned and blistered. And others, I just thought of Aimee with great love.

***

My mother watched *The Secret Storm* daily and called me nightly to comment. As her speech improved, her critical disposition returned. "Do you know that your hair was in your face all during the show today? And it's too dark... too blonde... you look like a floozy. That dress you were wearing made you look too fat... too thin. Your lipstick was too bright..." I took each and every contradicting statement to heart.

***

Frank and I had a little red Triumph Herald convertible now. When we drove to the farm for our monthly visits, we now arrived in style. Frank had been accepted into the family... kind of. Really, he was tolerated politely. He and my parents had nothing in common with each other; though, God bless them, they all tried.

Danielle loved being at the farm. My father took her around with him when he fed the animals. It was so wonderful to watch the two of them go off alone together holding hands, he having to lean down because he was so much taller. Sometimes they would take Otty the otter down to the pond so he could swim and zip around in the water. My father would help Danielle take off her shoes so she could wade in where the bank was shallow. When Otty swam over to nibble at her toes, as he had done with me, my father would lift her up just in time. She trusted him to take good care of her. She took for granted that he would keep her safe, never once doubting him.

***

I was making a lot of money now, what with the soap opera and the commercials. For a person who came to New York City with one hundred dollars in her purse, I was making enough money to stash away for a rainy day. In fact, I was making a lot more money than my husband, which was difficult on our marriage. The way I dealt with the money issue was by not dealing with it. "Here, husband, I don't understand any of this. Can you figure it all out?" And, of course, he did because he was and is good at that kind of thing. Working on a soap opera brought in thousands more than working on Broadway, even if the theatre you were managing was sold out every night; even with Edward Albee's *The Delicate Balance* and with *The Man of La Mancha*, starring Richard Kiley, which was to run for 2,328 performances and win five Tony Awards, including Best Musical.

Life is funny. Life is strange. Life just makes you shake your head sometimes in wonder. In May of 1968, my character Wendy Porter on *The Secret Storm* became pregnant after having a love affair with her stepmother's ex-lover. In July of 1968, Wendy Porter ran away from home on the verge of giving birth. In August of 1968, Wendy made one short phone call to her father and then she disappeared forever. On August 30, 1968, I gave birth to a son and we named him after his father, Francis Ernest von Zerneck, II.

Thirty-Seven

OH, SWEET LOVE

Francis, a.k.a. Franny, Fran, Frank, Frank, Jr., had white-blond hair that was so thick, like his grandfather Peter's, that I had to wet it down throughout the day so it didn't stand up tall and wave wild in the wind when we took him on his carriage rides in Central Park. Of course, our treasured son was covered with the same navy blue blanket with its gray silk lining that had protected his sister a few years earlier and his father a generation before, just as he was now expertly pushed along in the old navy blue pram. He was a very observant baby with his large hazel eyes, so like his father's. He liked to watch the autumn leaves fall. He liked the sound they made when I scrunched them in my hand as he sat in my lap and watched Danielle swing herself high and mighty. He liked the way the sunlight felt on his face and he called out to me if I parked his carriage in the shade. At night, while Frank was still at the theatre, Beatrice and Peter would come up to the apartment to visit. We'd take Franny and stretch him out on a blanket on the living room floor and, while Danielle slept peacefully in the next room, we'd hover over him, admiring every little bit of him. And that is another thing Frank's parents taught me: how to love, how to admire and how to share joy.

I was now on yet another soap opera, called *The Best of Everything*. Rona Jaffe had written the best-selling novel about four girls moving to and living in New York City the decade before. The movie had followed a few years later. Now it was to become a soap opera, and I was there from the very beginning, the first day of rehearsals. In fact, I was the first character to appear in the opening scene the day *The Best of Everything* premiered on television.

It was on this soap opera (produced by James Lipton, whom we got to call Jimmy; also a writer, poet, composer, actor and, later, host of the Bravo television series, *Inside the Actor's Studio*) that I met someone who would become my best friend for life. She was the only person I had ever known whose childhood rivaled mine in terms of instability, and we bonded immediately.

Patty McCormack had been working as an actress since the age of four. At one point, for two entire years in her young life, she had not only been on the Emmy award-winning television series *Mama*, which rehearsed during the day, but also, at night, she portrayed Rhoda Penmark, an eight-year-old sociopath and serial killer, in *The Bad Seed* on Broadway. She was nominated for an Academy Award for Best Supporting Actress for her role in the film version of *The Bad Seed* in 1956 and was also given a star on Hollywood's Walk of Fame.

***

The one thing we could all count on in life was the fact that it continued to change, whether we wanted it to or not. In 1970, Frank was offered a job as general manager of the Mark Taper Forum, a prestigious theatre in downtown Los Angeles where exciting new plays were being done. So we picked up and flew to L.A., where I got parts guest starring on television series and a running part on *General Hospital*.

Though the old 1920s Cape Cod house in the Hollywood Hills that we rented was the only thing I liked about season-less L.A., Frank loved every aspect of it. He sped around in the little red Triumph Herald, tan and handsome with the world at his feet. After working at the Mark Taper Forum for several years, he began producing movies and mini series for television. He worked day and night. He began to make twice, three times, twenty times as much money as I ever made.

Where I had mostly been able to manage my grief in New York, in L.A., isolated as I was, it took me over, flattened me to the ground. The *beast* began to appear again, more and more often. He was much louder now, much stronger in Los Angeles. I was mortified most of the time now. I couldn't trust myself. I wanted to drive off the side of a cliff. Jump from a forty-story building. Make it all go away. Forever. These feelings were made all the more frightening when contrasted with the pure happiness and love I experienced being with my two children and my husband. So, though my little family had become my foundation, this grief was a relentless wind that threatened to pull it all to shreds.

I became so angry about my life not being my own, that one day I took myself to get some help. Psychological help. This time it was not forced upon me. I was asking for it. I needed it to stay alive.

***

"I have everything. And yet..."
"And yet...?"
"And yet ... there is something absent."
Silence.

"I have many things. I have more than I need. And yet..."

"And yet...?"

"And yet... there is something missing."

"Missing?"

***

"I wonder why I wasn't stronger. Why didn't I say 'no'?"

"Why didn't you?"

"I was too weak."

"You were too weak to say 'no'."

"Yes, I was."

"Why?"

"Because I was just a child myself."

"Children say 'no'."

"Yes, they do. But I didn't. I never did. I never did say 'no'."

***

"I wonder what she's like."

Silence.

"She could be crazy. I mean, after all she was put through in the womb."

Silence.

"My womb."

Silence.

"Oh God. What did I do?"

"It's alright. Let it out. You're safe here. I won't let you hurt yourself."

***

"I have this beast. He comes and goes at will."

Silence.

"He's very powerful."

Silence.

"He has control over me."

169

Silence.
"I want to come and go at will."
Silence.
"I want to be the powerful one."

Julie, sidesaddle on Sea Witch, at the Devon Horse Show on the way to the ring

The man in the pinstriped suit. New York City, 1963

Acting composite, 1965

Julie and Frank on their wedding day, January 15, 1965, in Westbury, Long Island

TOP: Frank, Julie, Frank, Jr., and Danielle at Sunny Hill Farm
BOTTOM: Publicity photo for the ABC soap opera *The Best of Everything*
Clockwise from top left: Julie, Patty McCormack, Rochelle Oliver, Kathy Glass

PART IV

Kathy

Thirty-Eight

SEE? YOU HAVE NOTHING TO BE AFRAID OF

———————

Certainly, my brothers and I had been punished before—and yes, I knew better than to question the authority of an adult—but there was something clearly off-center about Gloria. I didn't trust her judgment anymore. Gloria's short fuse was easily lit and, without warning, would often ignite in a flash of explosive behaviors. I had remained silent about it for too long and decided it was time to tell my father what was going on.

I waited until Dad went out to the patio to smoke his after-dinner cigar. I knew Gloria wouldn't interrupt us as she didn't care for the 'stinky stogie' smell, so under the cover of smoke, I decided to fill Dad in on Gloria's alter ego.

"Dad, she's really mean," I whispered as we sat alone on the moonlit patio. He took a puff on his cigar, drew back his head, and with his mouth in an open pucker, blew three smoke rings.

"She hits us," I persisted. "I'm scared when you're not here."

"She hits you?" he asked.

"Not just me. Frankie and Jerry, too."

He took a long draw from his cigar and slowly blew out a stream of gray smoke.

"Listen, Kathleen," he said, placing the cigar between his teeth, allowing his words to escape from each side of his mouth. "She's got a tough job." I heard the Kathleen-just-needs-time-to-adjust tone in his voice.

"But Dad," I interrupted, "I'm afraid of her."

He reached for the ashtray and put out his cigar. Then he turned toward me, took my hands into his and gently whispered, "No one will ever replace Mommy. I miss her, too."

Before I could persist in my point, a fight broke out between Tracey and Jerry. They were in our line of vision—sitting at the kitchen table in front of the glass doors leading out to the patio.

"I'm the racecar!" Tracey hollered as she grabbed the Monopoly piece out of Jerry's hand.

"You called the shoe," Jerry protested.

"Liar!" Tracey screamed and did what she always did when she didn't get her way: yelled for Gloria.

Dad started toward the kitchen. Just then, Gloria came into frame, grabbed the duo's wrists and sat them side-by-side on the family room couch. Dad stopped and held his position in the doorway; I rushed over and stood beside him. *Ah ha! Now Dad will see the real Gloria for himself,* I thought.

To my dismay, Gloria diffused the quarrel as if she were Mary Poppins. Within minutes, Tracey and Jerry were back at the kitchen table laughing and passing 'Go'.

"See, Kathleen," Dad reassured me, "you have nothing to be afraid of."

Thirty-Nine

PARTISAN POLITICS

Gloria wasn't all bad; she did have days that made me want to nest in her arms and surrender to her care. The truth is, I very much wanted a mother, and most of the time I wanted *her* to be my mother.

Those were the days Gloria spoke in a soft voice imbued with Southern charm and sat Indian-style on the floor with her children, all five of us, and played hours upon hours of board games like Sorry, Trouble, and Clue. On those days her gait was fluid, a rosy glow glistening in her wake. On those days I could see a hint of my mother in her frame. *This is what Dad sees in her*, I would think on those days.

On other days we were invisible to Gloria; she'd sit consumed in her thoughts or throw herself into preparing mason jars filled with strawberry-fig jam that would find its way onto our peanut butter sandwiches day after day after day, until the last jar was emptied into the trash, often prematurely, when Gloria's back was turned.

One day, a day when we were invisible, Tracey and I decided to visit our friend Lisa, who lived one block away—a trip that required Gloria's permission.

"May we go to Lisa's house?" we purred politely. Gloria was perched over the kitchen counter perusing the latest issue of *Stitch and Sew*.

"What?" she asked without looking up.

We asked again with crossed fingers tucked behind our backs. "Yeah, sure," she answered as she turned the page.

An hour later, Gloria came out of her trance, and Tracey and I were 'nowhere to be found'. Frankie reported we had gone to Lisa's house. "You said they could go," he bravely reminded. "I did no such thing!" Gloria hollered and ordered Frankie to fetch us.

"You guys are in *big* trouble," Frankie warned on our brisk walk home.

As we headed down our street, we looked up to see a barefoot Gloria—her red hair, like flames, blazing out of her head. Her hands were fisted and her arms were curved at her sides: a posture that screamed *I'm gonna beat the shit out of you.* And that's exactly what she did—once we got home, of course. Tracey got it, too, which was shocking, as I had never seen Gloria raise a hand to either of her daughters. All attempts to explain ourselves were met with a thrashing more ferocious than the one before. Explanation and reason were futile when Gloria was in this state. I quickly learned the best defense during her violent tirades was not a good offense but a silent tongue and limp body.

On days when Gloria was not auditioning for the role of Carol Brady or that of Joan Crawford, she would wear an eclectic mix of moods on her sleeve. On those occasions she'd use her candy-covered words like *darlin'* and *precious,* dipped in a honey-tongued delivery, but her narrowed eyes and vinegary aura told us to put the armor on. On those days she was the most dangerous, and on those days the best defense was distance, out-of-the-house, next-town-over distance. However, sometimes we had no choice but to face the redheaded dragon.

One morning, after Dad left for work, Gloria insisted on preparing all of us breakfast before school. "No cold cereal this morning," she announced. "I'm going to make everyone a hot breakfast."

We sat like zombies in our bathrobes and bare feet, waiting at the kitchen table. Gloria was not a morning person and the thought of her getting up early to prepare breakfast was peculiar, weird even, and cause for alarm. Within minutes Gloria began to serve us, one by one, wearing a sugary smile.

"For you, Kathleen-a." She slowly, almost reverently, placed the morning meal in front of me.

When she was done serving each of us, she stepped back, crossed her arms, and stiffly leaned against the kitchen counter like a prison guard. She must have been unaware of the slow tick of her tapping fingers repeatedly rippling down her bicep, but I saw it, and read it like it was Morse code—*I'm in charge here*, she said with each tacit tap.

I must admit, I hadn't seen this one coming, and for a split second I tipped my hat to her ingenuity. The aroma of smoked sausage, scrambled eggs spiraled with cheddar cheese, and cinnamon buns bathed in white frosting radiated from the plates— well, Tracey and Melissa's plates. For her stepchildren, the menu boasted a healthier fare. My brothers and I were served lukewarm lumps of high fiber Ralston cereal carelessly heaped onto paper plates.

"Hey!" my little brother immediately protested. But before Jerry fell into Gloria's waiting snare, Frankie kicked his shin under the table and with big-brother authority mouthed the words "just eat it"—using the back of his head as a protective wall between

Jerry sitting across from him and Gloria standing smugly behind him.

" 'Hey'—what?" Gloria mocked.

Jerry dropped his head and held his tongue. The old me would have chimed in on Jerry's "Hey!" with a louder "That's not fair!" However, I remained calm and ate my breakfast, or rather, swallowed my lumps, in silence.

All of us—even Tracey and Melissa—were stunned at this display of partisanship and punishment, but, to me, their trapped words spoke with one voice. *They're on Gloria's side*, I thought. All traces of hope and security evaporated and resentment poisoned the air. We were now a house divided. It was us versus them.

Forty

SILENCE

I sat in my fifth grade classroom that same day, glad to be there, safe from harm, sheltered under the umbrella of clear expectations and wrapped in the warmth of Sister Peggy's lecture on the Treaty of Tordesillas. But it wasn't long before I found myself reliving the lukewarm-cereal morning in my head.

I'm going to tell Dad, I thought angrily. *She'll be sorry.* I had basketball practice after school and knew Dad would be the one to pick me up. *That's when I'll tell him*, I decided.

I was standing with a group of parents and teammates when Dad drove up. He rolled down the power window—a luxury in those days—and nodded a friendly smile to the other parents before rolling the window up again.

I didn't have to look at Dad to know something was wrong. He didn't say hello. He didn't get out of the car to talk to the other parents. In my twelve years of life, that had never happened. Dad lived for the impromptu, fifteen-minute conversation, and unless there was a five-alarm fire within sight, a quick nod just didn't happen.

"Did you have a good day, kiddo?" Dad asked as I got into his car.

"Yeah," I lied.

I needed a minute to figure this out. I focused on the air

conditioning vent on the dashboard in front of me. *Something's not right*, I thought as I stared at the horizontal slats. Fear seized me and for a brief moment, paranoia set in: *Gloria must have called him at work. Gave him another version of today's breakfast. Told him to expect a tall tale from me. And now, Dad is waiting, waiting for my big lie.* My eyes searched the dark abyss between the slats for the answers.

Suddenly, Dad pulled over onto a vacant shock of land overlooking the river.

"I need a minute," he said without a smile, his mind still elsewhere. He turned off the car, got out, and walked toward the river's edge.

"What's wrong, Dad?" I called out as I ran after him.

He twisted away from me and placed his hands on his head like an imaginary cap. The bend in his neck amplified the beleaguered look on his face.

"How did I let this happen?" he mumbled. "She's like a teenager out of control." His voice took on a nervous pitch. "She's gone through the savings—charged up every credit card. How did I let this happen?" I heard the anxiety in his expelled breath.

I had never seen Dad like this; even on the worst of days—the day my mother died—even then he had remained composed. But not today. Today, he was scared. My dad, my protector, my hero, was scared. His fear quickly transferred to me.

"Don't worry, Dad," I said, grabbing his hand, "it'll be okay."

A tear spilled from the shallow puddles forming in my eyes. He wrapped his arms around me, cradling my head close to his heart. After a few minutes, he pulled back and looked into my eyes, my wide-open eyes, waiting like a baby bird's beak for just a drop of assurance.

"Hey," he said, tracing my hairline with infinite tenderness, "we're a family. We'll get through this."

On the way home, I kept repeating *we're a family—we'll get through this* over and over in my head as if repeating it would make it true. But the gurgling in my gut prevented me from believing it, or even wanting it. If this was family, I didn't want a family. I wanted whatever it was I had before. I wanted peace.

I decided not to tell dad about the breakfast incident. Something inside me told me *not now,* and I was learning that my inner voice was smart and reliable.

When we arrived home Gloria was bedecked in a formfitting dress and an innocent pout, serving my dad's favorite: pork chops with mashed potatoes and baby lima beans. She reeked of guilt and manipulation. Dad and I both sensed it but said nothing. Instead, we went along with it; after all, *we're a family—we'll get through this* was still dangling from our lips.

Later that evening, after the dishes were dried and put away, after baths were taken, after homework was checked, the rumblings began. A slammed door, a raised voice, a louder retort. It was their first fight, or at least the first fight I had witnessed. The honeymoon was definitely over.

Gloria stormed out of the master bedroom, leaving an invisible trail of fire in her wake. "Where's my purse?"

Tracey rushed to help her find it. The rest of us remained motionless.

"Come on, Melissa," Gloria commanded.

And just like that, Gloria and the twins were gone.

***

The next morning, I awoke to the rattling of my brothers fixing bicycle tires in the garage, the giggling of the twins on the swing set, and the laughter of Dad and Gloria in the kitchen, scrambling eggs and toasting English muffins.

And so the dysfunctional relationship began. Gloria now had full control—control of the purse strings, the heartstrings, the puppet strings. In Dad's inaction, in his need to restore the calm, he had handed her all the power.

Dad was a Labrador, not a Doberman. It simply was not in his nature to growl and show his teeth. Instinctively, however, I knew that schoolyard bullies did not respond to reasonable dissuasion, and Gloria was just that—an overgrown bully. Our home had become her turf.

Forty-One

JUST A TRIM, PLEASE

It was 1975; I was twelve years old. My brothers and I had just come back from a restful summer in Philly, which felt like one long rejuvenating exhalation. I returned refreshed, filled with love—the kind of love that I could only get from time spent with my family, the type of love that fertilized my soul and allowed for full and long-lasting blooms. And blossom I did.

My legs seemed to grow several inches that summer; the baby fat cradling my face melted away, revealing contours of high, feminine cheekbones. Inside, I was still the same softball-playing tomboy, but my exterior was doing all it could to deny it. "She's lovely," strangers commented. "Kathleen is coming into her own," buzzed a circle of women at church. It was becoming apparent there was a female buried beneath the layers of tangled hair and sweaty smudges—and she was coming out, ready or not.

My coming out was not, however, welcomed by everyone. Gloria was less than pleased with the recent developments. I could tell by the impatient tone, which would strangle any conversation that gave birth to a compliment toward me. "Yeah, well, she's growing up," she'd say with a matter-of-fact lift of her eyebrows.

By the middle of my seventh grade year, Gloria had had enough. She and I were in the local grocery store one day, rounding the cereal aisle making our way to the condiments; I was relegated to the task of pushing the cart.

"My, aren't you a beautiful young lady," a frail woman with a hunched back and kind smile commented.

"Thank you," I whispered as I lowered my head and pushed forward.

A compliment within Gloria's earshot usually meant trouble for me.

I glanced over at Gloria scanning the shelf a few steps ahead of me. There was nothing about her stance that looked irritated; she hadn't heard the comment. But before I could digest the feeling of relief, the old woman walked over to Gloria, pointed at me, and asked, "Is that your daughter?"

My heart stopped. I squeezed the handle of the cart and winced my shoulders forward.

"Well," she paused, "...yes." Her hesitation spoke volumes.

"She's a rose," the old woman cooed. "And look at that beautiful head of hair." The well-meaning stranger could not have known of the thorns that would grow out of that comment.

I kept my head tucked, but in my mind's eye I could see the controlled chagrin on Gloria's face.

After the groceries were put away, Gloria called the twins and me into the kitchen. "Take a seat," she ordered.

"What's going on?" we asked.

She appeared with a stack of white bath towels and a black, oblong zipper bag. She set everything down on the kitchen table and unzipped the bag to reveal an assortment of scissors in ascending sizes, each with their own private pocket, and a long, narrow black comb.

"Haircuts," Gloria announced. "You're first, Tracey."

"I want bangs," Tracey said.

Melissa was next. "Bangs, please," she begged. "Just like Tracey." Tracey was the older twin—by six minutes—and Melissa, like most younger siblings, seemed to feel comfortable following Tracey's lead.

I was last. I sat on the barstool and draped the bath towel over my shoulders. Gloria stepped back and quietly examined me like I was a painting at an art gallery, tilting her head slightly to the left and then to the right.

"Just a trim, please," I said. I was particular about my hair—it was the one thing of which I had control.

"No bangs," I said. "They'll get in my eyes." I pinched my thumb and index finger together. "Just a half-inch, please."

"Uh huh," she mumbled. "Don't worry. I'll make you look nice."

She began to cut. I could hear the slow-motion snip of the shears close to my head. Too close. I watched a twelve-inch section of brown hair fall to the ground. Startled, I grabbed the side of my head to feel the effects.

"Not that much," I yelped.

"Relax," she smiled. "I know what I'm doing."

I pulled away and looked back at her.

"Just a trim!" I said, tears welling up in my eyes.

"Calm down," she ordered, as she squared my shoulders forward again. "I said I know what I'm doing."

Do I get up and run?

My hesitation cost me another section of hair. *Snip.* A cool presence now occupied the left side of my neck and felt like a window had been opened. *Snip.* My head felt lopsided now; weightless on one side, full on the other. *Snip.* The point of no return. I gave in to the moment. I had no choice but to give in.

"All done!" she said, as she stepped away with a pleased look on her face. I jumped up and ran to the bathroom mirror. Upon hearing my gasp, Gloria called out from the family room. "It's called a pixie."

I didn't recognize the girl in the mirror staring back at me. Gloria came into the bathroom and stood behind me, smiling, running her fingers through the short half-inch patches of hair.

"I wanted a trim," I whimpered.

"Oh, stop being so ungrateful," she barked, as she pulled her hands back. "You look fine, now go out and play."

I entered school the next day with my shoulders hunched and my head down, wishing I could disappear.

"What happened, Kathleen?" my teacher asked.

"My mom cut my hair."

"Well, dear," she said, "that's the good thing about hair. It always grows back."

Forty-Two

SHE'S A QUACK

After the haircut, Dad insisted that Gloria get some counseling. Surprisingly, she agreed. I overheard closed-door conversations about 'lithium' and 'manic depression' and hoped these mystery words would be the magic elixir to our problems.

We all attended family therapy one evening a month in a bare room with a stale odor, shoe-scuffed walls, and a laundry basket filled with dirty toys and *Highlights* magazines. The doctor with all the answers sat in a folding chair between the arms of two couches facing one another, four feet apart.

The entire experience was upsetting for me. I had done nothing wrong and was angry about being forced to go. Gloria, however, seemed to relish the attention. Like a publicity-starved actress, she turned on her charm during these appointments, especially drizzling her sweet syrup all over Frankie, Jerry, and me. During each session, I sat quietly, refusing to take part in her smoke-and-mirrors act. The dismay in the therapist's eyes was obvious as she watched the kind and temperate Gloria try to pull me out of my shell. *Kathleen is the problem here*, she must have thought. After a few months of one-word answers from me, the woman with an advanced degree asked to meet with me, one-on-one.

"You lost your mother at a young age. How does that make you feel?" she pried.

"I'm alright," I answered. *How dare she talk about my real mother?*

"How do you feel about your stepmother?" she continued.

"She's okay," I cautiously answered.

"She's okay?" she repeated.

"Well," I hedged, "we don't really get along anymore."

"Why not?"

"She gets mad at me a lot."

"What happens when she gets mad?"

I took a deep breath before I spoke. "She throws things. Hits me with her shoe, or her hand if she's barefoot." I inhaled again and continued. "Calls my real mother bad names. Calls me worse. Much worse."

A long gap of silence followed my confession as the therapist feverishly wrote on her yellow legal pad. Suddenly, I realized I'd pay dearly for this comment when Gloria found out.

"She's not so bad," I said, trying to fix my mistake. "I probably deserve it."

A week later, Gloria announced, "That therapist is a quack!"

And that was the end of family counseling.

***

After counseling, Dad called our parish priest. When that did not work, he took us on long vacations. Dad continued to look for ways to bring peace to our home. Nothing he did worked.

Forty-Three

YOU'RE MINE

Despite the issues with Gloria, the twins and I became friends, good friends. We shared clothes, talked about boys, and played on the same softball team. We fought sometimes, but our scuffles were never a problem unless Gloria stepped in.

One afternoon, Tracey and I were on the patio planning our next show. We had formed an acting troupe called The K-T Cats. On occasion, we would solicit Jerry and Melissa's participation, but for the most part, Tracey and I created and performed the shows debuted in the front yard for whoever happened to be outside playing. On this particular afternoon we couldn't agree on a dance move and an argument erupted.

"That's dumb!" I said.

"You're dumb!" she replied.

The growing volume caught Gloria's attention. "What's going on?" she asked as she stepped outside.

"She called me dumb!" Tracey yelled.

"Don't take that from her," Gloria replied. "Stand up for yourself."

Tracey stared at me, not knowing what to do.

Gloria prodded her again. "Come on Tracey, do something!"

Tracey took a half-hearted swing and missed.

I knew she didn't want to hit me. I knew this was all Gloria's doing. *Why can't she just leave us alone,* I thought.

Gloria pushed Tracey toward me. "Go on. Hit her."

Tracey swung again.

"You missed, fat girl." I didn't want to say that to Tracey; I didn't want to call her fat. I was just angry at Gloria. But by the hurt in Tracey's eyes, I could tell she had taken it to heart.

Wounded and angry, Tracey drew in a nostril-flaring breath. Her hesitation was like the deadly warning of a rattlesnake. I had no idea what was coming, but I knew whatever it was, it would be delivered with a flesh-piercing bite. She cocked her head back and hissed, "Well, at least I'm not *adopted!*"

Adopted? I wasn't adopted. What was she talking about? I knew it wasn't true; nevertheless, I saw regret in her eyes as the last word leapt from her tongue.

"I'm not adopted," I laughed.

Tracey looked over at Gloria, who shrunk back. And just like that, the spar was over. Claws retracted, revolvers holstered, white flags drawn.

"My mom died, that doesn't mean I'm adopted," I insisted. "You're the one who's adopted. Remember? My dad adopted you."

Both Tracey and Gloria, contrite and silent, stood motionless.

I walked to my room and sat on the edge of my bed. My heart was pounding and my mind was racing as I tried to figure out what had just happened. *There's no way I'm adopted,* I thought. *Dad would have told me.* A little while later, I heard the growl of Dad's car pulling into the garage. I walked stiffly out to meet him.

Dad knew immediately something was wrong.

"What's the matter, kiddo?" he asked.

My eyes locked onto his as I asked, "Am I adopted?"

He stepped back, his face tight with concern. It was in that moment that I knew—I knew it was true. I stood, frozen, afraid to move, afraid to continue this inquisition I had begun. My heart stopped, only to be restarted by the snap of fear pulsing through my veins.

"I thought Mommy told you," he said.

My throat tightened, and my stomach melted. He saw the shock of it all in my eyes.

"She didn't tell you?"

My mind shifted into rewind, back to a time when a beautiful blue-eyed woman tucked me in at night, when I was certain of who I was and from where I came.

"Frankie and Jerry are adopted, too. Mommy was supposed to tell you," Dad explained.

"She didn't," I managed to say.

"It doesn't matter, Kathleen," he said as he approached me, arms outstretched. "You're my daughter. I've never thought of you as anything else." His words burned like acid—it did matter. I was *not* his daughter... not really.

I remembered a time when I was four, shopping with my mother at JCPenney—she was looking for a dress. I ducked under the waterfall of polka dots and paisleys and hid in the center of the circular rack, only to become frightened and reemerge grabbing my mother's legs. Except they weren't her legs; they were the legs of a stranger. But for a few seconds I was deceived, deceived by a false sense of reality. Here I was again, hugging the legs of a stranger— completely unaware—and deceived for nearly twelve years by the same false sense of reality.

Or had I known all along I was adopted? Had my mother weaved it into her fanciful stories of angels sitting atop white clouds and I hadn't understood?

I felt Dad's arms wrap tightly around my shoulders, but I was numb. My light had gone out and I was nothing but a spectator; I pulled back and looked at his face—a face that resembled my father, but which was now somehow different, foreign.

I pushed him away, grabbed the door handle, and found myself back in the house, pinballing through rooms cluttered with memories that now seemed more like mythology than personal history. Everywhere I stepped I was reminded of everything I wasn't— anymore. The Australian pine in the backyard beckoned me, and I sat cradled in the gray shadows of its limbs.

My brothers, they're not really my brothers; my cousins are not my cousins; my aunts are not my aunts; my grandparents are not my grandparents. Then it hit me: *my mother, the mother I had loved, mourned, and longed for—she was not my real mother, she was never my mother.* A cold wind swept through my chest and made a graveyard of the special place once reserved for my memories of her. I wanted to sleep forever; I wanted to grasp on to the wings of an angel and fly far away; I wanted to be anybody but—

"—Kathleen," my dad gently squeezed my hand.

I looked up, startled.

"May I join you?" he asked as he pulled back his hand and crouched on both knees.

I inched closer to the tree, but nodded.

"You are my daughter, Kathleen," he started.

I pulled my knees to my chest and buried my face in the divide.

"Your birth mother wanted the best for you," he continued.

The thought of another mother both frightened me and drew me in.

"She loved the theater and wanted to become an actress. But she knew she couldn't do both. Couldn't raise you and pursue acting," he explained. "She wanted a stable life for you."

I lifted my eyes and rested my chin on my knees.

"The nuns said your mother was strong-willed," he paused, taking a minute to put his arm around my hunched shoulders. "I think you're strong-willed, too, like her."

I buried my face back in the gap between my knees and closed my eyes.

"I remember the day we went to the hospital to get you," he continued with a smile. "You were the loudest baby in the nursery. The nun lifted you from your crib, but you continued to wail."

I opened my eyes but kept my head down.

"The nun handed you to Mommy, and you stopped crying. You knew you belonged with us. We've never thought of you as anything but ours. No matter what, you are my daughter, kiddo."

I didn't know which hurt more, the fact that Dad was not my father or that my real parents had given me away. I couldn't bear the loneliness born of this thought, so I inhaled the cheerful vapors trailing from his words and lifted my head.

"I *am* your daughter," I said, baptizing my admission with reluctant tears. "I don't want to be anyone else except your daughter."

I fell into Dad's waiting arms. "You're mine, kiddo," he repeated. "You will always be mine."

Kathy growing up. LEFT TO RIGHT: Age 5, age 7, age 8, age 10, age 13, age 18

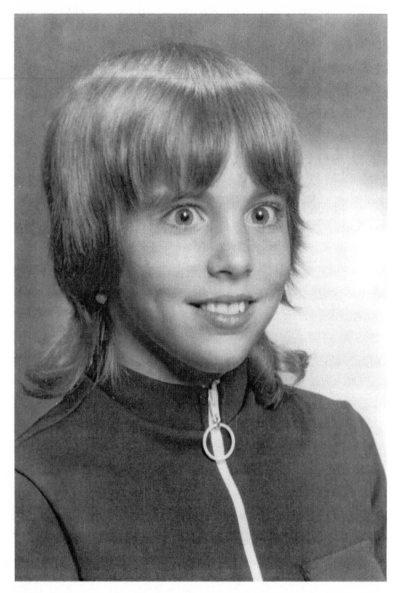

Still in shock, six months after the "trim"

PART V

Julie

Forty-Four

TIME COMES AROUND

Slowly, I began to feel more comfortable in Los Angeles, in my own skin, but still I craved New York. When Beatrice and Peter moved to L.A. and found an apartment very near our house in the Hollywood Hills, it became easier. We flew to Philadelphia at least four times a year to visit my parents and the farm and, when they could, they visited us. They loved our little house, surrounded by an acre of land. They loved that my towheaded son could run naked on La Brea Terrace, wearing only a cowboy hat and a holster with guns. They loved his stunt shows performed especially for them and Frank's parents, though all four were horrified when he'd tumble down under a table and emerge, his face totally covered in blood, having quickly smeared special effects blood "borrowed" from his father's sets. He loved hearing my father read *King Kong* to him, and he loved my mother's stories of her childhood. I was so happy that even though we lived at such distance from each other, he was able to get to know my parents and that both my children got to have the love of both sets of grandparents. I loved sitting back and watching it all happen. It was like time had come around and everything was right again.

And then, in April of 1977 my mother suffered a ruptured aneurysm, which sunk her into a month-long coma. I spent two weeks at her bedside before she died. The doctors assured me she could understand me. I hoped she could, because I talked to her the entire time I was there. I talked to her about my life and my children and her life and how remarkable it had been. There didn't seem much sense in raking over the coals again, despite the fact that they were still burning inside me. One day, I brought a pair of tweezers with me and plucked her eyebrows and a stray hair on her chin. I hope someone does that for me one day if I'm ever lying in a hospital in a coma.

Before I left to fly home, I told her, "I love you, Mom. I love you very much."

Forty-Five

TIGHT AS A FIST

My father was sitting in the living room, in his chair, waiting for me when I arrived. It was several weeks after my mother's funeral. Until then, I couldn't remember us ever being alone together for more than a few minutes at a time.

He was thinner than the last time I had seen him, even though he had Margret cooking and caring for him. The lines in his face were deeper. His blue eyes, which normally sparkled, were dulled and glassy.

"How was your trip?" he asked. His voice was drowsy. Spiritless.

"Fine," I said, placing a kiss on the top of his head.

He was sitting in his leather chair in the dark, with only the late afternoon light coming in through the window. Margret had not been able to get him to change his clothes for the occasion of my arrival. His shirt was bloodstained from feeding the animals, his pants were muddy and he looked like he hadn't shaved in days.

My father never published anything after my mother's death. My parents were tight as a fist, you see. I don't think they took too much notice of the outside world, except for the occasional required social event and a dinner party every few months. My father's seclusion was important if he was to write. My mother was the queen of the fortress, but the guardian, too. My father was the king. And that was the secret of their love. Together, they needed and wanted no one else. When the monsoons poured down and bathed them in mud, when the sun burnt pieces of their wings if they dared to soar too high, they had no need to venture out for help. They had each other.

So when I came along, I coasted on the air currents around them. Of course, I had people to take care of me, but as I grew older their privacy became less secure. When we finally settled down at Sunny Hill Farm, I was free to roam. And of course I did. And of course I roamed as close to my parents as possible. And of course I waited at the fringe of them to be let in.

Their muffled rumblings, in whatever mood, excited me, made my blood run fast, for they were the sounds of my parents vulnerable and unguarded. Limp with desire, I waited to be touched or held, and sometimes I would accidently brush by one or the other just to satisfy my need to make physical contact with them. To be read to for an hour each night as I lay on the Oriental carpet in their part of the house, in the 'big living room', in front of a roaring fire, and to be able to take in my father's full, rich tones, my mother's delicate beauty—was to fly to heaven on gossamer wings. It was my time alone with them, and it was worth everything to me.

***

I was sitting in my mother's chair now, facing my father. "How are you feeling?" I asked. "Are you sleeping at night?"

"I feel alright for an old man. And I sleep on and off," he answered softly. He kept crossing and uncrossing his legs and turning to look out the window. I could tell he was uncomfortable being alone with me. But as I watched him I began to realize that it wasn't so much that he was uncomfortable—more than anything, he was shy. Without my mother he was suddenly in the world all by himself. He didn't know how to converse one-on-one, without her around to deflect some of the attention directed at him. He didn't know how to feel without her there to tell him he was hungry and needed to eat, that he was tired and needed to sleep. He barely knew how to breathe in and out normally without her there to bear witness. He didn't know how to live without my mother by his side. He was terrified. And he didn't know what to do about it.

I tried to ask questions to keep the silence at bay, but he gave me one-word answers. I moved out of my mother's chair and went to sit at his feet. Then I just started telling him about my life. I talked about the children. I told him about a book I had just read. I talked about how exciting it had been, going up to the barn and jumping in the hay back when we had first moved to Sunny Hill Farm. We remembered Elwood, a local farmer, who would arrive on his tractor drunk out of his mind, wearing a black high hat and trumpeting a hunting horn, every New Years Eve.

"How about Frank?" he asked, after we had been talking awhile. I told him that he was about to start his fifth movie for television. He asked me whether we were still in touch with William Holden, with whom Frank and I had become friends after shooting a movie Frank produced in Germany called *21 Hours in Munich*, about the killings of the Israeli athletes during the 1972 Olympics. My father had been in the Navy with Bill and laughed at the fact that he and Frank now shared a mutual friend. "I never thought I'd say this, Julie, but I think you married a good man. And you travel all over the world together, just like your mother and I did. It pleases me to see you so happy." His words took my breath away. Tears welled up in my eyes. I sat there at my father's feet, and thought, *Oh dear God, thank you for this moment.*

Forty-Six

THE PHANTOM

We moved from the small house in the Hollywood Hills to a large white house on an acre of pure green, bordered on three sides by walnut trees in the flatlands of Toluca Lake in the San Fernando Valley. It was here that one evening we decided to tell our children—Danielle was twelve, Franny was nine—that they both had a sister. We gathered in the living room, so they knew something was up.

"Are you getting a divorce?" Danielle asked apprehensively.

"I really don't want you to get a divorce," Franny told us in no uncertain terms.

"We are not getting a divorce," we assured them. "It's something else."

They both breathed sighs of relief.

We plunged in headfirst.

"You have a sister that we have never told you about."

"We had her before we were married and gave her up for adoption."

"She is a year and a half older than you, Danielle."

"Four and a half years older than you, Fran."

"I can add," Fran said.

The room was quiet and went on being quiet for a long time. We had decided not to tell them about the mental hospital. What purpose would that have served? I knew we did have to tell them about the baby. I knew we did have to tell them because it was possible, according to statistics I'd read, that one day she could come knocking at our door. And then what would we say? *Oh yes, this is the sister we never told you about.* Would they ever trust us again after that? I doubted it.

"What is her name?" Fran asked.

"Aimee," we told him.

"But they've probably changed it," Danielle said. "I'm sure she has another name now."

"You're probably right," Frank or I said.

We had always thought of her as Aimee, so this is something that took us both aback for a moment.

Danielle was intrigued that she had an older sister. We later looked for her together during a televised choir program that came out of Philadelphia.

"Is that her? She looks like me but taller. She's older, so she could be taller. Look at her. She looks just like me."

Our son was not intrigued by the knowledge that he had another sister out there somewhere. Maybe he would have been if it had been a brother. I don't know. He was nine. Anyway, he liked the family as it was, he told us, just the four of us.

Every year on Aimee's birthday, April 19, Frank and I toasted her with a glass of champagne. But deep in my gut, despite the statistics, I pretty much knew she was gone from us forever. Even though I had left a letter with Catholic Charities about where I was if she wanted to find me, I most likely would never see her again. She had her own family now. Frank and I were only her birth parents. The parents who heard her first laugh, watched her take her first steps, they were her real parents. Nevertheless, we never stopped thinking or talking about her ourselves. She was forever with us, the phantom daughter and the phantom sister, who existed but was never seen.

***

"We've moved. It's nice. I'm glad we did it."
"What about the beast?"
"The beast? Oh him. I've been too busy hanging pictures to worry about him. So everything's good now!"
"Is it?"
"Yes, I think we can begin to wind down now."
"You mean to once a week?"
"Well, I was thinking once a month."
"All right."
"And then stop for a while."
"All right."
"I think I need a break."

***

"I thought I'd just check in."
"Is there something you want to talk about?"
"No, not really."
"Then things are going well for you?"
"No, not really."
"Do you want to talk about it?"
"No, not really."

***

"I told them. I told the kids about Aimee."
"How was that?"
"I thought it would be a relief."
"Was it?"
"No."
Silence.
"The beast is back again."

Silence.
"He's angry that I told them. He's making me pay the price."
Silence.
"Oh God. What did I do?"

PART VI

Kathy

Forty-Seven

THE MOUTH OF THE RAT

"We're moving to the mouth of the rat," Dad announced in the spring of my seventh grade year, the longest year of my life. The year I was scalped, the year I was orphaned, and now the year I would be plucked from all things familiar. We kissed our quaint, beachside community goodbye and headed two hours South to Boca Raton.

"Change is good," Dad quipped. I wanted to drink the Kool-Aid he was serving, but by then my taste buds had matured and I preferred the vinegary truth.

He was forthcoming about one thing, however: things were definitely changing. We moved into a one-size-fits-all community with narrow streets and short driveways. Most of the neighborhood dads drove trucks with big toolboxes and preferred blue jeans and rolled-up sleeves to my Dad's shirt and tie. "Your dad's a pencil pusher," the girl next door informed me a week after we moved in.

"I don't like it here, Dad," I moaned.

"You just need time to adjust," he replied

Dad was right; I soon discovered how warm and friendly our new neighbors were and was glad to have made the move. In fact, we all embraced the change. However, it was Gloria who responded most positively. Although she still experienced chronic fits of uncontrolled anger, she was more cheerful and accommodating in between. For the first time in years, our home was a place I wanted to be—until the day we received the letter.

I was the one to bring in the mail that day. I was expecting a letter from my best friend. "There it is," I said expectantly, as I reached for the white envelope. *To the Mother of the House,* it read. "Junk mail," I sighed.

"Mail's here," I called out and placed the envelope on the kitchen counter. Gloria, who was preparing dinner, looked up at me and smiled. "Would you please set the table?" she asked.

I was putty in her hands on days like this and immediately did as she asked.

After a few minutes, Gloria sat down on a bar stool at the edge of the kitchen counter and reached for the envelope. She read the letter, folded it closed, and sat quietly for a minute—then all hell broke loose.

"Goddammit!" she hollered, as she pounded her fist on the Formica.

She stormed over to the kitchen window and pulled back the curtains, looking left and then looking right.

"Goddamn neighbors," she roared, as she reached for two pot lids air-drying on a dish rack. "I'll show them!"

She charged outside into the backyard and broke the afternoon silence with the slam of her makeshift cymbals. "Mind—your—own—fucking—business," she chanted over and over.

Evidently, the envelope addressed to the "Mother of the House" claimed that Gloria's "...injurious explosions can be heard from several streets away," and according to this unidentified neighbor, "...the police will be notified if this violent behavior continues."

After receiving the letter, Gloria's entire attitude toward the move changed.

"I hate this goddamn place," she complained to my dad.

Dad tried to help her work through it, but she turned her anger on him.

"I'm going to go stay with Honey," she announced at the start of summer. "The twins are coming with me."

Gloria spent most of the next two months back in our hometown with her grandmother and daughters, coming back intermittently to pick up her mail and gather more clothes. I remember the Saturday morning she showed up unannounced as I was making pancakes.

"Make me two," she demanded as she put down her keys. "Tracey, Melissa, would you like some pancakes?" I heard her ask.

I could feel the resentment frothing in my gut like bubbles in a stream coming to the surface. "Yeah, right," I said loud enough to be heard yet soft enough to deny.

Gloria rose up like a King Cobra, flaring her hood. "Excuse me?"

I was familiar with her pre-strike posturing and took off running toward my bedroom. Gloria ran after me and stopped in my doorway. I backed up into the far corner and let out a yellow-belly call for my dad, who was in the backyard. She stepped toward me and immediately noticed my mother's framed face standing guard six inches away on my dresser.

She paused to pick up the picture. "Your mother was a bitch," she snarled, as she spit on the picture and threw it at me. Then she picked up my lamp, cocked her arm back, and aimed in my direction. Dad came in from behind and grabbed her arm. She turned, seemingly shocked at both his strength and his gall. "You both can take that dead bitch mother and shove her up your asses."

Dad's presence had reinvigorated my boldness. "Fine by me!" I snapped back in a voice loud enough to be heard, impossible to deny.

She shoved the lamp at Dad, pushing him against the doorframe and out of her way.

"I'm leaving you shits," she said as she began to pack her things. "I'll send the moving truck next week."

My brothers and I remained numb, afraid that believing it too quickly would cause it to backfire on us.

Dad, who was a devout Catholic, didn't believe in divorce, no matter the circumstance, and tried to reason with her.

"You don't understand," she told him as she slammed her suitcase shut. "I never loved you in the first place."

And just like that, she was gone.

This time, for good.

Forty-Eight

STATE OF MIND

Gloria had left us with one of everything: one chair, one lamp, one pot, one pan. But it didn't matter because she had also left us with one very important thing, peace of mind, and there is no need for creature comforts when you have an inner equilibrium that has been fine-tuned by ill fortune. My brothers and I possessed that first-trip-to-Disneyland high, and Dad, who was out of sorts at first, eventually came to terms with the divorce, and his regrets faded in the light of our relief.

With Gloria gone, I wasn't as uptight. I could now think about other things besides surviving from day to day. It felt good to just lie on my bed and dream about what my new life would be like. I could do anything I wanted; there was no one there to hold me back, no one there to criticize my every move. I didn't need to look over my shoulder anymore. For the first time in four years, I could breathe.

It was then that I could finally pull my feelings about being adopted from the mothballs and comfortably try them on. I was getting used to the idea of being an adopted child. It didn't scare me anymore, but I had questions that I wanted answered. I was nervous about talking to Dad about it and waited for the right moment to start this conversation.

Early one Saturday morning, I saw my opportunity.

"Why did Frankie's mom give him up?" I asked as I took a seat on the floor across from Dad, who sat in his red leather chair reading the newspaper, smoking a cigar.

"What's that, kiddo?" Dad asked as he raised his brows over his reading glasses.

"Why did Frankie's mom give him up?" I repeated.

"Well," he said, quartering the paper closed, "Frankie's mother was seventeen. She was a good student and wanted to go to college."

He paused and drew in a breath, but before he could continue, I blurted out, "What about my mother?"

"Ah, yes, your mother," he said. He was trying to slow down the pace of our conversation.

I knew I could be impetuous—especially with him. He was extraordinarily patient, and this was often both a source of frustration and of comfort to me. Today, it was simply maddening. For now, I just wanted answers I could chew on.

"Your mother loved acting," he said and then paused again.

"What else do you know about her?" I asked impatiently.

"I know from the nuns at the hospital that she named you Aimee," he continued.

Aimee, I thought to myself. The name sounded peculiar. Not like me at all.

"She was twenty years old," he continued.

"Twenty?" I pulled back in disbelief. "Then why didn't she keep me?"

I had assumed she was sixteen or seventeen and too young to take care of a baby.

"She wanted to become an actress. And she wasn't—" he hesitated.

"She wasn't what?" I pinched my brows together.

"—married."

"She didn't want me because she wasn't married?" I asked sharply.

Married or not, actress or not, a twenty-year-old should be able to take care of a baby, I thought to myself. It hurt me to think she could give me away so easily.

"Well," I said curtly as I stood up, "I really don't care."

But the fact was, I did care. I cared enough to be angry. I cared enough to be hurt. I wanted to know every detail of the life I had as Aimee. Even if it was a life with a 24-hour timeline, I wanted to know about every second.

I walked away, hoping Dad would stop me, hoping he would sit me down and force me back into a conversation I desperately wanted to finish. But my father was not wired that way. And so I walked away; I walked down the hall and into my bedroom, where I sat on the edge of my bed and tried to figure out what I'd do next.

"What's the matter with you?" a familiar voice shot at me from across my room.

I looked up to see Frankie leaning back against my dresser with his arms crossed in unison with his legs. His presence shocked me, and his tone told me I had crossed a line. The afternoon sun streamed through the lace curtains and lit up his large, blue eyes, which now looked like two loaded guns pointed in my direction.

"What?" I asked feigning annoyance, but feeling alarm.

"Stop this nonsense. *Dad* is your dad," he said with an unbridled firmness. "That's all that matters."

"I just want to know," I said defensively.

This was the first time Frankie and I had talked about being adopted.

"Don't you want to know about your parents?"

He uncrossed his arms and took a step toward me.

"I do know about my parents," he said. "I know that my dad is in the next room, and he is a good man. And I know that my mother, *our* mother, loved us. That's all I need to know."

"But—"

"No, Kathleen, that's it." There was an odd mix of sadness and loyalty in his posture as he turned and walked away.

Frankie was right. I had parents, good parents. Why did I want to know more about people who had thought of me as nothing but an inconvenience? I decided to borrow his state of mind until I grew my own and floated the notion that I had another mother out to a faraway island called 'Not Now.'

PART VII

Julie

Forty-Nine

PORTRAITS

In 1986, we four—my husband, my daughter, who was now acting, my son, a budding writer/director, and I—decided we wanted to open a family bookstore. We went to Prospective Booksellers School in Chicago. *Location, location, location,* we learned.

I got a job at a bookstore in Beverly Hills during the Christmas season. One day a man came in and asked me what my favorite book was. I had just been looking through a beautiful art book. It was priced at one hundred dollars. I pointed to it.

"I want forty. Wrap them and I'll send someone to pick them up in an hour."

I felt like I did the first time I walked out onto a stage. I felt like I did when I said my first line in front of a camera. I felt like I did when I felt successful, a long while ago.

We all agreed on some rules: our bookstore would be like our home. We would greet everyone as if they were coming into our house. No sale would be too small; a person spending ten dollars would be treated as royally as someone spending a hundred. Inside the store there would be a forest green carpet, dark stained bookshelves with nooks and crannies and a plush oversized chair to drape yourself over.

We would have antiques, too. Vintage bread bins and tea sets from England for the cookbook section, and old black typewriters and good heavy pens in the writing section. And we would have full antiquarian collections from England, of Shakespeare, Dickens, and Thackeray, as well as all the brand new books.

We named our bookstore Portrait of a Bookstore, because our logo was a portrait of the four of us in profile and also as a way to pay homage to a series of biographical films Frank had made, which we referred to as his 'portrait movies'. We hired a manager and six booksellers, but the four of us worked hard in our different departments. Frank, Sr. was the accountant and the sweeper of the front sidewalk, and I was the buyer, the decorator, and the cleaner of the store. Danielle bought the children's books and greeting cards. Frank, Jr. worked in the store forty hours a week and was in charge of ordering and displaying all the books from Black Sparrow Press, a publisher of avant garde literature.

We painted the front door bright red and hung a shiny brass knocker on it. On May 17, 1986, my forty-third birthday, we opened for business. Our first customer was Frank's dearest friend and lawyer, Tom Hoberman, who brought in his son on his shoulders. Tom and his family were big supporters of our new endeavor. From the beginning, we were a success. Since we were surrounded by Warner Brothers, Disney and Universal, our customers were writers, directors, actors, producers, and other neighborhood people. These people met and fell in love in our store. They got married and had babies, and brought those babies to our store and the babies learned to talk and walk and read there. People wrote in our store; they wrote poetry, plays and screenplays, some of which would go on to become well known. But many of our customers were everyday people looking for a good book or an interesting gift, and they came to us because they knew we would move mountains for them. I got great pleasure from every aspect of running the bookstore. I loved unpacking all the new books that arrived daily. I enjoyed touching them, feeling the raised print on their covers, leaning down to smell each one, turning to that first page and reading that first sentence.

***

"I don't miss acting at all."
"Really?"
"Yes. I don't think I could ever do it again."
"You don't miss it at all?"
"I love being a bookstore owner."
"What about the beast?"
"Oh, he's around. I guess he always will be. Something enormous would have to happen to get rid of him."
"What enormous thing would that be?"
"I don't know. Maybe a big old shotgun?"

***

Throughout this time, Frank made films in places like Germany, South Africa, Australia, England and India. The children and I were only too happy to accompany him when we could. While in India, Frank was working on a mini-series called *Queenie*, which starred Kirk Douglas and Mia Sara, who would become Danielle's close friend and her eldest daughter Martha's godmother. On the same set, we met and befriended the talented British film and stage actor, Leigh Lawson, and his wife, the evercharming Twiggy. Our families became close right away and anytime either of us visited the other's country, we always made certain to get together.

Starting in the mid-seventies, while Frank and I were on vacation in England, we rented a five-hundred-year-old cottage in the Cotswolds, in a village called Buckland, about a two-hour car ride from London. It had a brook running in front of it so it was aptly named Brookside Cottage. We rented it several times a year, and then one day the owners said if we wanted, we could buy it. The pound was down and the dollar was up. So we could and we did.

Here in this place, which, to me, was one of the most beautiful in the world, we spent so much time going for long walks through the rolling hills dotted with sheep, driving from little village to village searching for antiquarian books and one-of-a-kind antiques to bring back to the bookstore. We would sit in front of a roaring fire on icy cold nights, reading and talking and thanking our lucky stars that such a place as this was ours. Frank, Jr. woke up on his 21st birthday there. Danielle was married there to James Fearnley of Manchester, England, the accordionist of The Pogues, a well-known Irish rock band from London. They married there in the church, no more than two hundred feet from our cottage. The eight church bells rang for hours in celebration. Everyone in the village, including my best friend there, Mavis Keyte, and her daughter Heather, attended the reception, as did all the Pogues, James's family, and our friends and relatives from America. Our dearest friends, writer and comedian Michael Mislove (whom Frank knew since their Hofstra days) and his wife, actress Nellie Bellflower (who produced *Finding Neverland* and *Miss Pettigrew Lives for a Day*) were there in all their splendor. My grandchildren, Martha, long and blonde, and Irene, our flame-haired one, took their first steps at the cottage and played in the brook, making stacks of mud pies, standing almost naked in their little green Wellington boots. We were all simply happy there—very close to God there, roaming the hills and the valleys, listening to bird song, church bells from surrounding villages, and the sounds of our own voices.

***

"I found a place I feel good in."
"What is it like?"
"It's far away. It's in England."
"That is far away."
"I don't know anyone there."
"Is it lonely?"
"No. No one expects anything from me there."
"Do people expect a lot from you?"
"I'm no good with expectations. I always fail."
"Always?"
"Mostly always."
"Mostly always?"
"Well, sometimes I do. But not so much as I used to... anymore."

***

Though Brookside was the only place my melancholy did not prevail, I still had to be careful. If I kept things to myself and didn't force myself to talk to Frank or my dear friend Patty, I got in trouble. If I had half a glass of wine too much, I got in trouble. If I got to feeling useless, ineffectual, inadequate, I had to be careful. It was a constant job, being careful, and sometimes I succeeded at it and sometimes I didn't. When I didn't, that bugger of a beast returned and there was all hell to pay. Somehow, however, I managed to keep him out of the lives of my children and grandchildren.

They were busy. Busy with their own lives. And I took pride in their accomplishments. In the early '90s Danielle produced and starred in a movie called *Living in Oblivion*, which went to the

Sundance Film Festival. Frank, Jr. wrote and directed a movie called *God's Lonely Man,* which also was accepted at Sundance. And Aimee... how I wished I knew what Aimee was doing.

Fifty

LETTERS

Life raced on like a train, winding and zigzagging through mountains of days, months and years. After my mother died, my father wrote to me weekly throughout the remaining years of his life. He typed out two to three pages on his old Royal typewriter telling me the news of his days, how the animals were, how he was, and sometimes sending me clippings concerning local news events. In one letter, he told me about a friend of his called Mel, a pet store owner, who was going to jail for importing drugs in the bellies of tropical fish from South America. In another, I learned that two hundred members of the Ku Klux Klan had marched in West Chester, and there had been a big riot. He told me about how he and Margret had gone out in the middle of the night in their pajamas during a ferocious snowstorm and saved twin lambs whose mother had died giving birth. He wrote:

> We have the two of them on the open oven door, thawing out. I am taking turns with Margret feeding them milk with a little whiskey in it from a dropper every few hours. It's nice hearing their baaahing every so often; nice to know they are both alive. I imagine they will be running around the house soon getting into all sorts of trouble. Margret has named one of them Lamb Chop. Hope that doesn't mean what I think it does.

When the postman would arrive I knew immediately when there was a letter from my father. He had been using the same envelopes with "Sunny Hill Farm, Malvern, Pennsylvania" engraved on the back for decades. I took my time opening each letter and then some more time reading it. I wanted each one to last for as long as possible. I wrote back weekly, too, and had been for years, telling him about Danielle and Fran.

> Danielle got into NYU, so she'll be living in New York and get to visit you more.

> Fran is making another video movie today with his friend Christian and I caught them jumping off the pool house roof into the pool. I'm glad they aren't both dead.

> Today at the bookstore we had a signing for Gore Vidal, (he says to say hello) and a week from now we're hosting another one for a self-published author no one's ever heard of. I hope people show up.

> Frank, Jr. got a nice little baby python today; about ten feet long. He's calling him Wolfgang. I assured him we would not be raising mice to feed him. And we would not be picking up roadkill on Hollywood Blvd., either.

***

When my father became ill, I traveled to Pennsylvania more often, and Frank, Jr. or Danielle would come with me. We sat by him, and gathered around him by the fire in the living room, he in his green leather chair, we on the Oriental carpet, and went over piles of old scrapbooks together. They were big, heavy, brown leather things containing bits and pieces of our families' lives. His grandparents' lives, his parents' lives, his life with my mother, and, more recently, pictures, cards and newspaper clippings from the lives of my brother and me and our children. My brother, his wife, and their daughter Alexandra (my nice niece, as I like to call her) took very loving care of him. My father adored Alexandra. At an early age, she read all of the *Wizard of Oz* books just because he loved them so much, and they had long discussions about the various characters and plot points. She made him laugh with her encyclopedic knowledge, which was very much like his had been at that age.

When my father died, we all flew together from Los Angeles to Philadelphia, my husband, my son and daughter and my daughter's husband. Even my granddaughters, Martha and Irene, were there. My brother and his wife arranged the funeral, and it was beautiful. It rained buckets, though. We all stood under our black umbrellas as he was laid to rest next to my mother, his mother, Pretty Polly Perkins, and his grandmother. A man among women.

***

On the airplane ride home, I took out my father's old Royal typewriter. I was bringing it home with me. I set it on my lap tray, opened it up and began to write. *Click, click, click.* This was no soundless computer. *Click, click, click.* The sound of it reverberated through the small cabin. *Click, click, click.* This was no hushed-up apparatus. The sound of it echoed the voice of my father. Time had moved on and I was made old by a sound I loved so much.

LEFT: With Patty McCormack in fake furs. London, 1980

RIGHT: Julie and Frank on set in Munich, 1976

Frank on set in the south of France, 1985   In Cape Town, South Africa, 2005

ABOVE: Daniel P. Mannix, IV with Tod, who inspired *The Fox and the Hound*
BELOW: Portrait of a Bookstore celebrates its 25th anniversary

ABOVE: Brookside Cottage, The Cotswolds, England
BELOW: Granddaughters Martha and Irene with their father, James Fearnley,
in the garden at Brookside

Frank, going for a walk on the Cotswold Way

PART VIII

Kathy

Fifty-One

MAN CUB

By the time I turned sixteen, I had put the strife of my past behind me. I felt alive and hopeful and ready to believe, once again, in the angels of my youth.

It was most likely those very same angels who sent a gust of wind up the school stairwell into my open locker, blowing some papers out of my hands and into the path of Bryan Hatfield. I had noticed Bryan a year earlier, walking down the crowded school corridor. I had only caught a glimpse of his profile but was drawn in by his sun-kissed skin, the lift in his shoulders, and the spiritedness in his walk. And now here he was, stooped over, three feet away, about to touch the very same papers I had held just seconds before.

"Are these yours?" His voice was assured and inviting. He was wearing tan surf baggies and a bright orange t-shirt with an ocean wave silk-screened on the back. He glanced over at me as he gathered the papers, now at his feet. He wasn't anything like the jocks I had dated before; he was small-framed and lanky, and looked like an older version of Mowgli, the man cub from *The Jungle Book*. But his presence stirred something undeniable inside me that I had never felt before.

He stood and smiled. He was taller than I remembered. Almost six feet. He stepped toward me and asked again, "These yours?"

"Yes," I blushed. He smelled clean, like fresh linens and cut lemons. The warmth in his mahogany eyes put me in a trance. I wanted to grab the papers out of his hand, throw them back into the wind, and push him up against my locker where I could kiss him forever. But instead I said, "Thanks," and turned away, unnerved by his effect on me.

He stood there for a few seconds before I felt him turn and walk away. I shoved the ruffled papers back in my locker, slammed the door, and spun my lock again and again, chiding myself with each spin: *Why didn't I talk to him? What's wrong with me?!* Bryan was a graduating senior, and I was only a sophomore. With the school year ending in a few days, I knew I had spoiled my only chance for a date with him.

***

That summer I spent almost every day at the beach, where my friends and I would coat our bodies with baby oil and squeeze lemon into our hair. We went for long walks, played Frisbee in the surf, and lounged on our colorful beach towels laughing at something that happened at a party the night before. *I love my life,* I'd say to myself as I drove to the beach each day.

One day, I arrived at the beach just after dawn and well before my friends. I lay down on my towel and read a little F. Scott Fitzgerald. The rhythmic sound of the waves crashing on the shoreline made my eyelids heavy, and before I knew it I was facedown and asleep on a rain-soaked Gatsby as he reunites with his beloved Daisy. I'm not sure how long I was asleep before I felt an imposing presence in the sand next to me. I jerked my head back and squinted crossly into the sun.

"Sorry for waking you," a familiar voice spoke.

It was Bryan, the mahogany-eyed man cub. I pulled myself up on my elbows and tried to speak, but the words froze in my throat, so I smiled and gestured 'hello' instead.

He laid his surfboard on the dune and sat on the edge of my towel. "Do you remember me?" he asked. The ocean water glistened in his dark brown hair, occasionally sending a bead of saltwater down his bronzed chest and disappearing into the blue of his baggies.

"Yes," I managed to say. I had never been shy around a boy, but he was different. His proximity to me tied my tongue in knots.

"You want to get breakfast?" He spoke easily, as if we'd been friends for years.

"You don't even know my name," I said, forcing the words from my mouth.

"Kathy," he said. "You're Kathy Wisler." He stood up and reached for my hand. "I'm Bryan Hatfield. Let's get breakfast."

From that moment on we were inseparable. By the end of summer, we were head-over-heels about each other.

Fifty-Two

TEXAS-SIZED PUMPKIN

I knew something was wrong the second Dad walked through the door. His necktie was loosened, his sleeves were rolled up, and he was carrying a lidless box filled with files.

"I was laid off today," he said.

"Laid off? What does that mean?"

"It means I don't have a job anymore."

"You can find another job, right?"

I could feel him drawing strength from the trust I had in him and the simplicity of my solution.

Money was already tight, as Dad now had to pay the lingering debt left behind by Gloria, legal fees from the divorce, and child support for the twins.

"Why do you have to pay child support for someone else's kids?" I indignantly asked the day Dad signed the divorce decree.

"They *are* my kids; I adopted them," he said without resentment.

I could now see how his philosophy had impacted *my* life. It's what kept him from giving my brothers and me back after our mom died. Public opinion of the early '70s would have given Dad the green light to walk away from us. *How can he be expected to raise three young children—children who aren't even his—on his own?* they would have justified. But my dad was a man of commitment, despite the personal cost.

***

Over the course of the next six months, Dad spent his days mailing out resumes and going on interviews and ended each night with the hope that he'd be an employed engineer by morning. I began to chip in for the bills after getting a job selling shoes at the local mall, and Frankie, who had graduated high school and enlisted in the Navy, sent money home when he could.

The severance pay and unemployment didn't last long, and Dad, who had a degree in physics, had no choice but to take on two part-time jobs: one mopping floors at a convenience store and another delivering newspapers.

"It's just for a little while," he'd quip as he left for work each evening.

His positive attitude was just a front, however. I knew he ended each night on his knees praying for help. My room was next to his, and I could hear his muffled pleas through the wall: *I can't do this alone! Please, God, help me!* Could he have known I was praying the same prayer just a few feet away?

But the help never came, and six months turned into one year. And one year turned into two.

The pressures at home began to take their toll on me. I found myself worrying about everything from Jerry's homework and laundry to having enough money to pay next month's electric bill. Only Bryan, whom I had been dating for a little over a year, knew how desperate our situation had become. My other friends, most of whom came from wealthy Boca Raton families, had no idea of the realities I faced at home. I hid my misfortune behind lighthearted conversation and a swirl of activity. My life had become one continuous storm, and my feigned positive attitude an umbrella to keep me sane through it all.

But the umbrella was wearing thin—as on the morning I awoke to an incessant tapping coming from the living room. We had had a violent storm the night before, with thunder so loud it set off a car alarm down the street. *Tap. Tap. Tap.* I rolled over and covered my head with my pillow. *Tap. Tap. Tap.*

The unrelenting noise became unbearable; I flung my pillow across the room and stomped down the hallway into the living room. I gasped when I looked up. Rainwater had leaked through the roof and was now dripping from a saucer-sized opening in the ceiling onto the carpet below. I hollered for my dad, and we spent the next hour ripping up the carpet and stuffing old newspapers and towels into the hole in the ceiling. That was all we *could* do, as there was no money for a more permanent cure.

Later that morning, I called Bryan. He had become my go-to when things got bad. "I need to get out of here today," I told him.

It was late October and the rest of the world was getting ready for Halloween. "Let's go pick out a pumpkin," he suggested.

An hour later my troubles evaporated behind me, as Bryan and I strolled through the pumpkin patch, hand in hand, sipping cider, looking for the perfect pumpkin. Spending time with him was my way of recharging and I was thankful to have him in my life, but I sometimes took my frustrations out on him.

"Let's get that one," he said, pointing to an over-sized pumpkin the size of Texas.

"Are you kidding?" I said, releasing his hand. "It's too expensive."

"I got it," he smiled.

"How can you spend thirty dollars on a pumpkin that's going to end up in the trash next week?" I asked, not wanting an answer. "Just take me home!"

The stress from problems at home was making me short-tempered and cold. That night I tossed and turned for hours and prayed for an imaginary sinkhole to open beneath me and swallow me whole. *Bryan stays with me out of pity,* I thought. I knew what I had become: a short-tempered she-devil with nothing to offer.

The next morning I called him. "We need to talk," I said with a distance in my voice.

"Yep," he agreed. "Come over tonight after you get off work."

He wants this too, I thought. I could hear it in his voice.

I spent the day wishing things were different, wishing that, for once, something in my life would work out. That evening, I headed to his house. *I'm not going to cry,* I thought, biting my lip as I turned into his driveway. His home, set back from the street, was surrounded by an oasis of tall trees, beds of leafy greenery and tropical flowers. As I drove up his dark, winding driveway, I noticed a flickering light in the distance.

What's that? I thought.

And then I saw it. It was the Texas-sized pumpkin, glowing brightly atop his car. He had carved I LOVE KATHY! across the front and thumbtacked a note underneath the words.

I laid my head on the steering wheel, heartsick, humbled, taken aback. After a minute, I got out of the car and reached for the note.

Dear Kathy,

You're 'it' for me.
I'm not going anywhere.
Now, come on in. I've made your favorite dinner: Chicken
Parm.

Love,
Bryan

That was the night I knew I loved him.

Fifty-Three

ON MY OWN

A week before I graduated high school, our lives hit rock bottom.

"We're going to lose the house," Dad said.

"Why?" I asked, as if I didn't know.

"We're behind six payments," he explained. "The mortgage company was going to give me a second mortgage to catch up, but—" he stopped and drew in a breath.

"But what?" I prodded.

"Gloria's still on the deed."

"What's that mean?"

"She has to agree to the second mortgage."

"And?"

"She won't," he said. "She's remarried now, and her new husband told her not to."

I didn't know which I should respond to first—the news that we would soon be homeless or the fact that Gloria was remarried, or, better yet, that she still could pull the strings attached to our lives.

The following month, we rented a U-haul, packed all of our belongings inside, and moved to the other side of town into a small, two-bedroom apartment. It didn't feel like home, but it was a roof over our heads and we were grateful.

The move and all the issues surrounding our situation left me feeling frightened and vulnerable—a feeling reminiscent of my years with Gloria, a feeling I hated.

With high school behind me, I realized I had no solid plan for what to do next. For the past two years, my focus had been on paying next month's bills rather than on my future. It was time for me to think about what I wanted to do with my life rather than let my circumstances define me.

Six weeks later, I found my own apartment with two roommates and enrolled in college.

"I'm sorry I can't help you right now," Dad apologized.

We had gone through our college funds during the Gloria era, and I could see the regret welling up in his eyes.

"I can figure things out," I assured him.

With that, I began a life completely on my own.

***

Although I lived paycheck to paycheck, I managed to pay my share of the rent, car insurance, tuition, and the rest of life's necessities. To my surprise, life on my own was much easier.

Dad's luck also changed. He found an engineering job two hours away, and every month he would send me a twenty-dollar bill folded in a handwritten note. I knew the sacrifice mired in the threads of that twenty-dollar bill; I knew he had fallen behind with his child support and was making inflated payments to catch up; I knew that twenty-dollar bill was a week's worth of lunches for him, and, each month, I debated mailing it back. But I couldn't. I knew rejecting it would tell him "I don't need you anymore"—and that wasn't true. It would never be true.

***

It wasn't until my junior year of college that I finally started to see a clear path for my future. I imagined myself wearing smartly cut business suits, sporting a leather satchel, working as a high-level manager for IBM or Johnson & Johnson. I envisioned an unencumbered life, which allowed me to travel from one big city to the next and to make enough money to live, finally, without worry.

Marriage and family were not part of that plan. However, Bryan, whom I had been dating since high school, remained a big part of my life. We had an undeniable chemistry, which made our relationship uncomplicated and worth continuing. I knew he was "Mr. Right," but I also knew it wasn't the right time. By the end of that same year, it was clear to me that he saw things differently.

It was Christmas Eve. I had spent twelve hours on my feet selling shoes to a frenzied mob of last-minute Christmas shoppers and was finally home, lying on the couch with my swollen ankles propped up on a pillow, watching *It's a Wonderful Life*. Both of my roommates had gone home for the holidays, and I was waiting for Bryan to come over to help me decorate my Christmas tree.

I heard a knock at the door.

"Come in," I called from the couch.

Bryan was dressed to the nines, wearing a navy-blue Brooks Brothers blazer, a striped oxford shirt, and gabardine trousers. He had a single red rose between his teeth—in one hand he held two crystal flutes and in the other a bottle of Dom Perignon. "Merry Christmas!" he said, smiling through the thorny stem.

He sat down beside me, popped the cork, and filled the two flutes. A warm feeling filled me as I thought of all the Christmas Eves we had shared before this one. He smiled as he handed me the champagne. I drank in his delighted expression, his warm eyes, his natural zest for life—an energy I had noticed from the very beginning, a buoyant spirit that had stabilized me during stormy periods.

He leaned over and kissed my forehead. It was a soft, slow kiss—a kiss that one remembers because it's given with such tenderness. He drew back and, reaching for my hand, got down on one knee. My heart began to pound. I felt my breath in my ears. I knew what this was—I had seen it happen in movies, I had read about it in romance novels.

He took a small, velvet box from his jacket pocket and slowly opened it, revealing a diamond ring.

"Will you be my wife, Kathy?" he asked, his eyes swollen with affection.

I sat up and looked at the ring and then back into his eyes, now wet with emotion.

"Oh, Bryan," I whispered as I drew back my hand and placed it over my mouth. I sat mute, paralyzed by the enormity of the moment.

"Well?" he asked.

I dropped my head in my hands and cried. "I can't. I'm not ready. I'm just not ready."

My unpredictable childhood had engendered in me a deep-rooted need for independence. I had to know I could thrive on my own before I could fully commit to a life with him—and that meant finishing college and starting a career first.

In the back of my mind I thought, *he loves me; he'll wait.*

I was wrong.

Bryan moved away six weeks later. We remained friends, but he eventually found a new girlfriend and seemed to adjust, rather quickly, to a life without me.

The months that followed were saturated with second thoughts and sad love songs. My three simple words, *I'm not ready*, had become like links in a chain binding me tightly to my desire for independence, but at a cost I was finding too dear. But I had experience with handling disappointment; when I realized it was really over, I sent my memories of him out to one of those far-away islands.

***

I graduated college in 1986 and accepted a position with a stock brokerage firm in the business district of Boca Raton. My new job threw me into more mature social circles, and soon I was dating men with an opinion about art and an appetite for accomplishment. I had long given up any fantasies about marrying Bryan, and although I felt hopeful, I realized with each date I went on that he would be the one I would never get over.

With school behind me, I had more time to spend with my family. One weekend, I learned Frankie was headed home on leave from the Navy, so I left work early that Friday and drove the two hours in hopes of surprising him. However, the surprise was mine when I pulled up to an empty house.

Although I was glad to be home, I was taken aback by the odor of dirty socks and stale pizza as I walked in the door. I dove headfirst into cleaning. I started with the sink full of dirty dishes in the kitchen, slowly worked through the family room and then on to the bathrooms. I peeked into Dad's room but quickly pulled the door shut when I saw the mess.

Dad was a mad professor of sorts, with his own way of organizing; when we had lived under the same roof, I was banned from cleaning his room. "You'll mess up my system," he'd say each time I tried to straighten things. His system was to heap all his clothes into laundry baskets and store every receipt, important paper, and gum wrapper containing his fingerprint in the dresser drawers. At age sixteen, I found it easy to look the other way. Now, at age twenty-two, I had difficulty restraining myself.

If I clean out a few drawers, I thought, *I can put some of his clothes away.* I opened the top drawer and started to organize the sea of papers: a Chinese take-out menu, an Ace Hardware receipt for 2-inch nails, a checkbook from a defunct Savings and Loan, a crumpled birth certificate.

"Goodness," I said aloud. "This should be in a safe deposit box."

I laid the certificate on the dresser and smoothed it with both hands. This was no ordinary birth certificate. It was a covert document with the parents' names obscured by the swipe of a thick, black marker. It was a document that had, by the look of it, been handled repeatedly. And what was even more compelling, it was mine. The birth date read April 19, 1964. But the name listed was Aimee's. The same Aimee I had discovered as the result of a fight with my stepsister some ten years ago.

I examined it closely: Aimee Veronica Mannix. I pronounced it aloud. Completely. Slowly. Cautiously. The sound of it saddened me. It was a name meant for someone else's daughter, a name never meant for me. I folded it up, stuffed it between the Chinese menu and the Ace Hardware receipt and put it back in Dad's drawer.

I spent the next hour sitting outside on the porch steps, thinking of Aimee's family, the Mannix family, while I waited for my family, the Wisler family, to arrive home. The thought of being adopted made me feel vulnerable—a feeling I hated, a feeling I had worked hard to avoid, yet a feeling I had to learn to live with.

My dad and brothers finally arrived home, but by that time, I was gone—at least emotionally. I still wrapped my arms around them when I saw them, still laughed at my dad's latest stories, still enjoyed my time with them, but there was a sadness inside that weekend that took me months to finally come to terms with.

***

I had come to terms with most of my life's misfortunes on the day I got the call.

"Hey, Kathy. It's Bryan."

I hadn't heard his voice in a while and hadn't realized how much I had missed it.

"You got a minute?" he asked.

"Yes, of course—more than a minute," I quickly answered.

"Radar died," he said with a shaky voice. Radar was his beloved Doberman Pinscher, whom Bryan had bought within a week of our first date; I knew the bond they had shared and could feel the heartache in his voice.

"What happened?" I asked. "He was only six."

"Someone let him off his run. I found him a few miles away, under an oak tree. The vet said he ran himself to death."

I started to cry.

"He really missed you after I moved away," Bryan continued.

His words were laced with kindness and reminded me of all the reasons I had fallen in love with him. "I missed you, too, Kathy," he said with an audible softness.

I didn't know how to respond; I knew he still had a girlfriend. *He's emotional right now*, I reasoned.

"Can I ask you something?"

"Yes," I said.

"Are you ready yet?"

Fifty-Four

NON-IDENTIFYING INFORMATION

We were married on a brilliant Saturday morning in January of 1988. Although surrounded by over one hundred friends and family members, it was as if we were the only two people in the church as we looked into each other's eyes and said *I do*. I had married my prince; he had returned to me with the glass slipper and found it a perfect fit.

We rented a modest apartment in a community filled with young couples just like us. Each day seemed a gift to be unwrapped and enjoyed. We even took pleasure in the routine that soon formed: sharing a cup of coffee before work each morning, knocking elbows in the kitchen as we prepared dinner each evening, watching *Seinfeld* on Thursday nights, ending each day with an excitement for the next.

One year later, we found ourselves in the hospital delivery room holding our baby daughter, whom we named Amanda. It didn't take me long to realize what I held in my arms: my child, yes, but she was more than just that. She was the first blood relative I had ever known and the only glimpse I'd ever have of my birth family, Aimee's family. As if by a gravitational force, I was drawn into her atmosphere. I saturated my senses in the scent of her skin, her cooing, her cries, and every nuance of movement.

My career took a back seat to Amanda's infant carrier, now strapped securely in its place. I had never imagined myself as a stay-at-home mom, but now I could not imagine myself in any other role. I eagerly traded my world of adult conversation and happy hours for a life filled with dirty diapers and sleepless nights—and considered myself lucky to have made the switch.

Several years later, I gave birth to our second daughter, Kathryn. She was one of those babies every mother wishes for—she slept through the night, she ate her peas and carrots, and she brought a calmness to our home that we had not known before. Her compassionate nature was never more apparent as on the day I received the news of my Aunt Annie's death. I hung up the phone and cried like a baby. Kathryn, only two at the time, sat with me, rubbing my back and wiping my tears with her soft, little fingers.

There was nothing more important to me than my family, and I knew Bryan felt the same. I watched the years of love and patience he had afforded me grow to include our daughters. He read them a chapter from their favorite book each evening; he helped them with their science projects; he taught them how to surf. Like my own father, he was fully present for them.

As our daughters grew, I marveled at the emerging clues to my past. The characteristics in them that I didn't recognize, I attributed to the genes of Aimee. Bryan and I both had brown eyes, yet Amanda's were a brilliant blue: *my birth mother was blue-eyed,* I rationalized. Kathryn was extraordinarily agile: *my mother was a ballerina,* I surmised. Both girls were precocious and imaginative: *my mother's penchant for acting is showing through,* I concluded. Like a scientist formulating an ongoing hypothesis, I observed every suggestion of difference in them and fleshed out my mother in the process. *This is enough,* I said to myself.

And it *was* enough until the day our neighbor's son was diagnosed with Mitochondrial disease, a genetic disorder. I began to wonder about diseases my mother may have passed down to me. That was the day I decided to write a letter to Catholic Social Services in Philadelphia, requesting information about my medical background.

I was surprised by the wave of guilt that washed over me as I dropped the letter in the mailbox. It felt as if I was betraying my dad; it felt wrong; it felt duplicitous. *I don't want to find her,* I assured myself, *I just want information.*

Three weeks went by without a response. Each day I checked the mailbox, and each day I was met with disappointment. Finally, after a month of waiting, I picked up the phone.

"Hi, this is Kathy Wisler Hatfield," I said. "I requested medical information four weeks ago. I am calling to follow up."

"Yes, Kathy—Wisler—Hatfield," the female voice answered, repeating my name slowly.

I imagined a woman with black glasses perched on the tip of her nose, sitting at a desk piled high with manila folders. Each of these folders harbored the secret identity of thousands of Aimees, now scattered like seeds blown off a dandelion and carried by the wind to far off places. I heard the rustling of papers as she talked.

"We've been short-handed this month," she explained. "Oh my! Here it is!" she said abruptly. "I remember this one."

"What—why?" I nervously asked.

I'm the product of a rape, I immediately thought.

Suddenly, I didn't want to know anymore.

"I've changed my mind," I gasped into the receiver.

"Oh, sweetheart," the kind voice on the other end said. "It's not bad news. It's interesting, *very* interesting; that's all."

"Really?" I asked, breathing in a sigh of relief.

"Young lady, you come from a fascinating family," she said matter-of-factly. "I can't give you their names, but I'll send you the Non-Identifying Information. It'll go out in tomorrow's mail," she promised.

Three days later, a large white envelope from the Archdiocese of Philadelphia arrived in the mail. Bryan was at the beach with our daughters, and I was glad to open it while alone.

Wanting to remember this moment, I held the envelope in both hands before slowly slicing it open and pulling out two papers. I scoured each word on the first page, which was a form letter outlining the steps to initiate a search. The second page, a document titled 'Summary from 1964 Records', took my breath away.

SUMMARY FROM 1964 RECORDS		
Birth Mother		**Birth Father**
	AGE	
20		23
	RACE	
White		White
	DESCENT	
English/French/Irish		German
	RELIGION	
Roman Catholic		Jewish
	MARITAL STATUS	
Single		Single
	EDUCATIONAL LEVEL	
High School + 2 Years Drama Classes		3 years College
	OCCUPATION	
Actress		Actor
	DESCRIPTION	
5'4", 105 lbs., slender, blonde hair, pug nose, fair complexion, beautiful teeth, wide deep forehead, oval-shaped face		5'6", 150 lbs., black straight hair, brown eyes, ruddy complexion, oval face, nice looking
	SPECIAL APTITUDES	
Acting		Singing, dancing, acting
	PERSONALITY	
Outgoing, pleasing, "A little girl trying to be sophisticated"		Not Given
	FAMILY	
52 years old, English/Irish descent, Protestant, College Grad, Writer	FATHER	German, Jewish, Actor Educated in theatre
48 years old, French, Roman Catholic, housewife	MOTHER	Theatrical agent, College Grad
Brother, 16 years old, High School Sophomore	SIBLINGS	Not given

The columns of information overwhelmed me. I had only envisioned a mother—the thought of having another father frightened me.

I reread his information again and began to create a persona for him.

Special Aptitudes: singing, dancing, acting. *He's gay,* I immediately thought. *That's why she wasn't married. They were cast in the same play—summer theatre,* I reasoned as I calculated the month I was conceived. *For her it was first love; for him it was an experimental fling; for me it was bad timing,* I concluded.

As I read about my birth father's family, I realized how deeply entrenched they were in theatre. Not only were my father and grandfather actors, but my grandmother was a theatre agent.

My birth father is in his fifties now, I estimated. *He may be on TV or in the movies.* I fleshed out a face with the details: black, straight hair; brown eyes; 5'6". *My father is Dudley Moore, or Danny DeVito, or maybe he's Dustin Hoffman.* My mind darted wildly; the possibilities made me dizzy.

I closed my eyes and envisioned their scenario: I saw tears spilling from my mother's naive, blue eyes as she is rejected by her gay, Jewish lover the day she reveals she's pregnant. Her English father and French Catholic mother tell her she has disgraced the family, and she is met with yet another form of rejection. Feeling abandoned and alone, she turns to the nuns at Catholic Social Services and is cared for by them until I am born. Knowing she cannot care for me on her own, she leaves me behind and starts a new life—a quiet life with a reliable man in a predictable town where she will live out the rest of her ordinary life.

I now had all the answers. I expected to feel complete, or, at the very least, satisfied. Instead, I felt sad, overwhelmed, and responsible. I was the reason for the blue-eyed woman's demise, the reason she would never achieve her dreams, the reason she would live a life in the shadow of her mistake. I was the mistake.

I slid the papers back into the envelope and filed it away, forcing it into hibernation, affording me the energy to move forward with my life.

Fifty-Five

THE CALL

I got the call on a pleasant, spring afternoon.

"Hey, kiddo."

"Hi, Dad," I said. We called one another daily. Some days we had a two-minute conversation, on other days we spoke for hours.

Today, however, was different. There was an awkward hesitation after my greeting.

"What's wrong?" I asked.

"Listen," he said, "I want you to sit down."

"Dad, what's wrong?" I had been seated, but his request drove me to my feet.

"I don't want you to worry," he hedged. This had been his way. If there was bad news to deliver, he did it slowly, while I impatiently tried to pressure it out of him in one squeeze.

"Dad, you're scaring me. Just tell me!"

"I have," he took a minute to clear his throat and then started over. "I have cancer."

Cancer. I knew this word. Intimately. In my eyes, cancer was a battle that could not be won; it was a war with a calculated outcome; it was the remainder of a life portioned off in stages: surgery, chemotherapy, and suffering. Each step doubled in duration and brought the victim closer to his or her own mortality. I felt the wind escape from my lungs, and my knees buckled, sending me to the floor.

Over the course of the next few weeks, Dad underwent MRI

and CT scans and fluoroscopy until the dossier revealed what we feared the most: he was terminal. There was no drinking from the cup of denial on this one; he had only a few months to live. With both sides of my intelligence, I put together a plan for Dad's remaining time. I took a leave of absence from my new job as a mortgage broker, arranged for hospice, and moved Dad in with us.

It was decided that Dad would take Kathryn's room. "I hope you don't mind," I said, pointing up at the Winnie-the-Pooh border.

"I wouldn't have it any other way," Dad joked. We were open and frank with one another, and I was glad for it.

April was Dad's strongest month. He was able to go for walks on the beach, play checkers with his grandchildren, and enjoy long conversations with friends and family members. Each evening before bed, he was treated to a live theatrical performance by Amanda, who was seven, and a neck massage from Kathryn, who was three. His spirits were high, and for a short time, we had hope the doctor's diagnosis had been wrong.

By May, however, his enemy tightened the vice, taking away both his appetite and his ability to hold down a meal. By Memorial Day, he was bedridden. A life once buoyant and assured had descended into a compound of pain medication and misery. I arranged for a hospital bed so we could rotate his frail body, but nothing could relieve the discomfort on his numbing limbs.

"I just want to stand," he would say after lying in bed all day. Each evening, Bryan would lift his gaunt body out of bed and hold him in a standing position for a few minutes. "This is glorious," Dad would say.

The end of June was washed in an ominous hue.

"No detectable blood pressure," reported the hospice nurse.

I could see the distance in his eyes. I sat by his bedside, holding his hand, telling him of the day's events in an attempt to keep him anchored to me just a little bit longer.

By July 1st, Dad had slipped into a coma. "Today will probably be the day," the hospice nurse warned. That afternoon, after putting Kathryn down for a nap, I sat on the edge of Dad's bed, adjusted the collar of his pajamas, and tucked the blanket in around him. "You were the best dad I could have ever had," I said as I stroked his cheek. "I hope you know how much I love you. Goodbye, Dad," I whispered, as I kissed his forehead.

I had imagined that, just like in the movies, I would sit by his bedside as he peacefully passed. But life does not always imitate art. His death was not peaceful. It was not graceful. It was anything but. After my goodbye, a brackish fluid suddenly began spilling from his mouth, and he began to choke. I pulled him forward and cradled him tightly in my arms. "I've got you, Dad. I've got you," I repeated. And as suddenly as it came on, it stopped, and then he was gone.

I have never cried so deeply, so gutturally, as I did that day, for I had never loved so deeply, so gutturally, as I had loved my father.

Kathy in high school

Sisters: Kathy in Indialantic at 18   Danielle in Hollywood at 18

ABOVE: Kathy with Bryan, on their first date
BELOW: A kiss from Bryan for graduation

LEFT: Disney World, 1998, with Amanda, Kathryn, and Bryan
RIGHT: Kathy dancing with her daughters

Kathryn, Bryan, Amanda, and Kathy today

PART IX

Julie

Fifty-Six

MIDDLE AGE

Like everyone else, Mondays through Fridays are Frank's and my working days. After breakfast we go our separate ways. He goes to his office dressed in his pinstriped suit, where he sits in front of his roll-top desk, maroon walls covered in framed posters of all the movies he has produced through the years surrounding him. There are over one hundred and fifty. He is so proud of them, so thrilled that he has been able to make each of them; they are in a sense all his babies. The phones ring all the time and Nancy, his assistant, answers them as they come rolling in. Emails appear on the large screen of his computer. He sips his coffee and tilts back in his leather chair. He reads several books and dozens of magazine articles a week, and still he has someone else he pays to do three times as much reading as he is able to. His film company is always in search of the next project to produce. He has breakfast meetings at Art's Deli, lunch meetings at The Bistro and sometimes dinner meetings at fancier restaurants. He is always working.

He loves his work. Sometimes he flies off to make his movies in distant lands, on far off continents, and lives in hotels for months at a time. No matter how beautiful each place is, it eventually becomes what he calls a 'Paradise Prison'. He is always missing me. So sometimes I go with him. No matter where we are, we get up before dawn, wrap ourselves in scarves, sweaters, down jackets, things we discard during the day as it heats up, and go to the set. He knows he's one of the luckiest men in the world, and he never takes it for granted. He is doing what he has always wanted to do, what he's dreamed of doing since he was a little boy lying on the cot behind the living room couch in his parent's one bedroom apartment in the Bronx.

For me, every day is Christmas because Portrait of a Bookstore receives packages of books and gifts every day. I am never lonely. I have a staff of seven and all my customers to keep me company. I write early in the morning or late at night. I write short stories, poems and novels. I write only for myself. Fridays, I go to an afternoon movie with Frank, Jr. Being a writer/director he needs to see everything—the good and the bad. Several days a week I pick up one of my granddaughters from school, and we go out for tea and a pastry and a chat. Danielle and I are on the phone a lot, and we meet up at the bookstore. She has moved on from acting to producing movies.

Weekly, I see Dr. Henry Neilson, a tall, lanky, gray-haired man, with deep crevasses aged into his sun-torn face. He is the age my father would have been and is quite renowned in his field. In his over-heated office, surrounded by shelves of eagle feathers and ancient relics from India, I lie on his couch, covered in a heavy blanket. I close my eyes, and he puts me into a dream state. In this state I am taken back to the day when I saw Aimee for the first and last time. "We are all connected. Always. Talk to her. Just talk to her," Neilson reminds me. I do. I talk to her. I tell her I hope she is happy. I tell her I love her. I beg her to find me. Half of me feels foolish doing this every time. Half of me believes that she can somehow hear me.

Six o'clock is when Frank and I meet up again. We sit in our back garden, in our over-stuffed outdoor chairs, the dogs asleep at our feet, and have martinis as we talk about 'the affairs of the day'. We can talk forever, just the two of us; we never run out of conversation, even after all these years. We talk about his day, the ins and outs of it, the ups and downs of it, and then we talk about my day. Sometimes we are out in the garden for several hours. It's our time together, and we know by now how precious it is. Then, Frank cooks dinner. I am the one to clean up.

Sundays are our best days. We have breakfast in bed and read *The New York Times*. We take the dogs for a hike in the Hollywood Hills. We go for a swim. Then we begin laying things out for Sunday dinner. That's when the children come over. Danielle, Frank, Jr., James, Martha and Irene. We set up outside. A blue and white tablecloth on our glass table near the grill, silverware, the good glasses, cloth napkins in silver rings, flowers, candlesticks, all under an extra wide umbrella. The doorbell rings, and in they come with bags and hats and sweaters and books that take over the kitchen. The house begins to flow with chatter and excitement. We all talk on top of one another. Frank and I exchange smiles. We drink. Frank grills. We eat. The sun goes down. We hug and kiss our offspring, and they leave.

Frank and I clean up and talk. We turn off the lights and go up to our bedroom and get into our pajamas. Our bed is big and white, covered with down pillows. We sink into them. We have been together for almost half a century. We know each other's habits and finish each other's sentences. Two French doors on the far end of the room are open to let in fresh air. We reach for our books and begin to read. After a while, when Frank's head begins to tilt down, I get up, walk over to his side, take off his glasses, put his book away, turn off his light and kiss his dear forehead. Then I go back to my side and kneel down. *Thank you,* I pray. *Thank you for all that you have given me. But please, one more thing, just one more thing. Please bring Aimee back to me.*

PART X

Kathy

Fifty-Seven

LEAVE IT ALONE

By 2007, our daughter Amanda, creative and eloquent, was a freshman in college, pursuing a degree in creative writing. Kathryn, in the thick of the middle school years, had thrown her energy into soccer and academics. Both girls were intelligent and beautiful and filled Bryan and me with tremendous love and pride.

Life was a mix of grocery lists, soccer shuttles, and piles of dirty laundry neatly separated into temperature-driven piles. I was a high school English teacher now, and my afternoons were spent grading papers while keeping our busy household running smoothly. Such was the afternoon, when an insurance auditor stopped by to complete a review on our home, a half an hour before I had to pick up Kathryn from soccer practice.

"May I see your homeowners' policy?" the auditor asked, after he shook my hand.

I hope this will be quick, I thought, as I looked at my watch.

I grabbed the file from the cabinet and returned to the kitchen, where he was crouched beneath the sink inspecting the pipes.

"I'll leave the policy on the counter," I said.

I opened the file and was startled by what I saw. It was the Non-Identifying Information from Catholic Social Services that I had received over ten years ago. I took it out and looked at it for a minute. I hadn't really thought about Aimee in years. I didn't want to lose this again, so I placed it on the computer desk in the kitchen and continued on with my business with the auditor. Within fifteen minutes, I was shaking his hand goodbye and heading for the soccer fields.

Later that evening, I sat at the computer to check my email and noticed my birth information on top of the printer. I studied each detail in the document. It said Aimee's grandfather was a writer; *maybe he wrote for a newspaper in Pennsylvania*, I thought.

I think I'll Google a few things.

I typed in the keywords 'Writer Mannix Pennsylvania' and clicked on the first site to come up. It was a *New York Times* obituary for a Daniel Pratt Mannix, IV. Mr. Mannix, the author of *The Fox and the Hound*, was 85 when he died in 1997. I did the math: *this man is the same age as the writer-grandfather on my document*, I thought. At the end of the obituary, it reported he left behind a son and a daughter, named Julie.

Next, I typed in the keywords 'Julie Mannix' and selected a link to the Internet Movie Database. IMDB is a website which summarizes, among other things, the professional experiences of actors. I read the site in disbelief. The Julie Mannix now lit up in front of me was an actress with a career dating back to the '60s, the decade in which I was born. The site revealed she was married to a producer named Frank von Zerneck, and together they had two children, also actors, named Danielle and Frank, Jr.

Can finding her be this easy? I thought. I searched the name Frank von Zerneck. Like a ravenous wolf, I scavenged the multiple websites under this name, devouring each detail and quickly looking for more.

According to the first few sites, Frank von Zerneck was a Hofstra-educated actor. His father was also an actor, and his mother a theatre agent—a detail that stopped me dead in my tracks. I scanned the document from Catholic Social Services again. Like a puzzle, all the pieces were seamlessly coming together.

Within minutes, I was reading an article about Frank and Julie von Zerneck's daughter, Danielle, born in December of 1965, eighteen months after my birth. Danielle had been an actress on *General Hospital* back in the '80s: Lou Swenson, the character of John Stamos's girlfriend. *My goodness*, I thought, *I scheduled my college classes around that show*; but the twenty years that had passed prevented me from remembering the character's face. I read on; Danielle had also starred in a variety of movies during the '80s and '90s, including *La Bamba*.

This can't be them, I thought.

Could it be that, with very little effort and within fifteen minutes, I had not only found my birth mother, but had also discovered my entire birth family?

No, I told myself, *it's not possible*.

A swirl of confusion whipped around my head. In a split second, my mind dashed back and forth, holding opposite positions.

I worried that I might have opened Pandora's box.

It's them, something inside me asserted, *and they're fine without you. Leave them alone*, this little voice insisted. *She married my father. Had two more kids. Left me behind. Why didn't she keep me? Why was I given away?*

Suddenly, I was aware of our differences, and I cringed at the pity they would feel toward the child they had named Aimee.

She's quite ordinary, they would say with a tsk-tsk in their voices.

My insecurities strangled the energy of the moment but couldn't beat down my strong-willed desire to know the truth.

I summoned Bryan from his Monday night football armchair to tell him what I'd found.

"Kathy," he said, "it's not them. Don't do this."

"But look," I said, pointing to the evidence. "It all lines up."

"I don't want to see you get hurt; leave it alone."

I saw the halo of good intentions circling his words, but I couldn't ignore the perfectly trimmed branches of this family tree. I took Bryan's advice, however, and left it alone.

A week went by, and I found myself thinking about it again. I just couldn't shake the synchronization of the details. I decided to buy one of Danielle's movies.

"Look," I said to Bryan, as I replayed her scenes repeatedly. "We have the same smile, the same face, the same way with our hands."

"You can see yourself in anyone if you look close enough," Bryan argued.

I decided to call my brother Frankie and tell him what I had discovered.

"I wasn't looking for them," I kept saying as I revealed each detail. I worried that he would become angry with me. This was an act of betrayal; I could read his thoughts between the telephone lines.

"What should I do?" I asked.

There was a long moment of silence. I heard him breathe in through his nose and shuffle his feet on the floor. *This is where he is going to tell me I'm selfish and ungrateful*, I thought.

He cleared his throat and said, "Dad's gone; there's no one that can be hurt by this. You should contact them."

The next day, I wrote Julie and Frank von Zerneck a letter. I wanted to give them the opportunity to walk away without feeling they had hurt me, so I worded the letter as if they were not the family of Aimee but as if they may know the family I was seeking.

I held the letter for two weeks before mailing it. Finally, on a Monday morning in late November, I sent the following certified letter:

Dear Mr. & Mrs. von Zerneck:

How do I start a letter such as this? Well, I think I'll simply just start with... I was born on April 19th, 1964, in Philadelphia, Pennsylvania. According to my adoption papers, I was given the name Aimee Mannix before I was placed for adoption through Catholic Social Services on May 16, 1964. My adoptive parents renamed me Kathleen Marie Wisler. Based on the documents Catholic Social Services provided me, I find it plausible that you may know some information concerning my birth family.

Attached are adoption documents from the Archdiocese of Philadelphia/Catholic Social Services. Would you please take a minute to look them over? It is possible that you may know some information that may lead me to this family. It is not my intention to disrupt their lives; I simply want to connect on any level they feel comfortable.

Please, at your convenience, let me know if you can assist me with additional information.

Sincerely,
Kathy Hatfield

PART XI

Julie

Fifty-Eight

BEING FOUND

Late one evening in 2007, twenty-one years after Portrait of a Bookstore had opened, just around Thanksgiving, I came home after a twelve-hour day of cleaning and shining and rearranging every glorious shelf.

I was exhausted. I poured myself a glass of red wine and fell into the closest chair, which happened to be one of four surrounding an old round pine table in our kitchen; that's where our housekeeper, Irma, piled up all the mail when she brought it in each morning. I put my aching feet up on the chair next to me and took a sip of wine. Tilting my head, I rested it on the back of the chair.

Frank was on the phone in his office, not too far away. I could hear his voice, firm and strong, so I knew he must have been talking to someone about work.

My eyes wandered to the stack of mail on the table. On the top lay a very official-looking certified envelope. It was covered with postage stamps and a stamp-stamp with a signature scribbled after it. I reached for it and picked it up. It was heavy.

Oh God, I thought, *I hope this isn't trouble.*

I set the heavy envelope aside so I could still see it but I didn't have to look at it if I didn't want to.

I reached for something simple. Something that I knew I could handle. Then, inexplicably, I changed my mind. Something inside me stirred. I set the envelope down. I reached for the hazardous piece of mail that had been signed for. I opened it. My heart started thumping. Little did I know this was the most important letter I would ever receive in my life. Little did I know this letter contained my resurrection. Little did I know this letter would change my life forever.

I slid out the papers inside. There was a typewritten letter on the top. Here is how that letter began:

Dear Mr. & Mrs. von Zerneck:

How do I start a letter such as this? Well, I think I'll simply just start with...

"Frank," I called out. "Frank," I called out again. "Frank," I called out again but louder. "Frank, Frank, Frank," I screamed.

And then, suddenly, he was by my side.

***

Kathy, I thought to myself. *Her name isn't Kathy. It's Aimee.* My arms were numb. My legs wobbly. Frank and I had come upstairs to my office to make our call to Aimee together. In our haste, we had forgotten the letter with the phone number downstairs in the kitchen, and I was on my way to retrieve it. As I began to descend the stairs, my legs buckled under me. I fell and I fell and I fell until I reached the bottom. And that's where Frank found me seconds later. I looked up at him with tears in my eyes. "I didn't expect it," I said to him. "I just never expected this. I don't know if I can handle it. What if it's not her at all? Let's not call her. Maybe we shouldn't call. I couldn't bear it if it's not really her. But she has the chart, so it has to be her. How else would she have gotten the chart? I don't know. I'm so confused. What should we do?"

"If it's not her we'll deal with it then. We're together. We can handle anything. And if it *is* her..."

"Yes... if it is her... Frank, that would be a miracle."

PART XII

Kathy

Fifty-Nine

HELLO?

"Hello?"

"Is this Kathy?" a female voice inquired.

"Yes, this is Kathy."

"Hi, this is Julie Mannix," she continued. "I received your letter, and I have some information for you, but before I tell you, could you tell me a little bit about yourself?"

Her voice was warm and crisp and spirited—like hot apple cider on a nippy November evening. I corralled my thoughts, which were ready to run wild with assumptions, and inhaled a deep, calming breath before I spoke.

"I was born in Philadelphia and given up for adoption as a baby, but I think I mentioned that in the letter," I said. "I had wonderful parents, but my mother died when I was six."

I heard a gasp on the other end.

"Oh my," the sweet voice sighed.

I continued with a synopsis of my life, and when I was done I heard the words that I had never imagined I'd ever hear in this lifetime.

"Well—" the articulate and expressive voice paused. "I'm your mother."

I will never forget that moment for as long as I live. I was standing in Kathryn's darkened bedroom, looking out the open window, running my fingers along the hemmed edges of the long white sheers. The fragrance of white jasmine floated in on a cool, stiff breeze, and silver moonlight spilled over the backyard. The enormity of the moment left me speechless. I closed my eyes as a brilliant mix of euphoria and tranquility exploded within my chest.

"I want you to know one thing," she said. "I—" she hesitated. "We—" she paused again. "We did not want to give you up."

Her voice was perfect, custom-made for my ears. I wanted to hit the record button in my brain and save this all for later. Half of me was listening to her words, but the other half was mesmerized by the melody.

"Your father is here, and he wants to talk to you, too. May I put him on?" she asked with a natural politeness.

"Yes, please."

"Kathy," he said. His voice was alive and full of warmth. "Julie and I could not believe it when we got your letter."

"It's wonderful to hear your voice," I responded softly.

"After you were born, I bought your mother a ring and had your birth date inscribed inside. She's worn it every day since."

I melted into each word and wondered if I was imagining all of this.

"We have celebrated every birthday," he continued. "You have a sister and a brother; they've known about you for some time now."

He paused for a second and then said the words that every adopted child wants to hear.

"I just want you to know," he said gently, "you were loved all along."

I didn't cry; instead, I became fully present in the miracle of the moment, a moment of trust and tenderness that I had supposed would never be mine.

We exchanged email addresses and promises to send pictures.

"Let's take our time getting to know one another," my mother suggested.

"Goodbye," I said, softly, regretfully, not wanting the call to end.

"Goodbye, dear daughter." And then she was gone.

I stood with the receiver still at my ear for a few minutes. It had all happened so quickly and I needed a moment to take it in. I was surprised at how effortless it was. It should have been an exhausting conversation, yet it was easy and left me feeling alive and loved and assured.

"Who was that?" Bryan called out as I walked into the kitchen and hung up the phone.

I sat in the red leather chair next to him. I leaned back, smiled, and taking a moment to find the right words, I said:

"It was them."

***

My doubts started a week later.

They're expecting Aimee. I'm not Aimee. I can't be anything like the Aimee they imagined me to be, I worried. *What if I'm not as easy to love as the baby they gave away? What if this doesn't work out? What will I tell my daughters? What will I tell myself?*

Sixty

WIRED TO HOLD A GRUDGE

"You keep saying you're okay with everything."

"I am."

"You're not."

Leave me alone, I want to say, but I narrow my brow at him instead.

"See," he says, "you're angry."

I had sought counseling a month after I found them. Bryan had suggested I talk to a professional about my feelings. This was my third visit.

"I'm not angry," I say with a willful laugh in my voice. He leans back in his chair and waits for the break in this circular conversation. "She was forced to give me up," I continue. "She could have aborted me."

We sit in silence for almost a minute; I can hear the tick of the clock hanging on the wall above my head. I notice his socks are unmatched—one black, the other a dark navy—and suddenly I am provoked by his gall. *Who is he to tell me I'm angry*, I think to myself, *when he can't even match his own socks?*

"I'm happy," I say, this time without the laugh behind it. "She's wonderful. Besides, I'm not wired to hold a grudge."

He hands me a pen and legal pad, turns and walks toward the door.

"Write your mother a letter. Tell her everything you'd tell her," he pauses with a backward glance, "if you *were* wired to hold a grudge."

I sit alone.

I pick up the pen. It's heavy and black and opulent.

Dear Julie, I write.

~~*Dear Julie,*~~ *Dear Mom,*

I was there that day. I felt your hand cradle my head. I felt your breath on my cheek. And then I felt you turn and leave. You left me. Alone. You left me behind. I trusted you. And then... you left me.

Was it because I was not blonde? Would you have stayed if my eyes had been blue? Were my dimples not deep enough? What would it have taken to get you to want me?

I should have been yours. I should have seen the world through your eyes, by your side.

I would have been good. I would have behaved. Eaten my vegetables, cleaned my room, said 'please' and 'thank you'. I would have made you love me. Somehow.

But you left me. And went on to build a life without me. As if I didn't exist. That's what hurts the most. You were better off without me.

All I ever wanted was to love you. I would have loved you like no other. You broke my heart. You never gave me the chance.

Until now. Now we have a chance.

Your daughter,
~~*Aimee*~~
Kathy

PART XIII

Kathy (and Julie)

Sixty-One

DOUBLE DOORS

My cab pulls up in front of the Ritz Carlton hotel. It's been nine months since I first spoke to the von Zernecks, and ten steps and two sets of doors are the only things that separate us now. After months of taking things slowly, exchanging photos, emails, and talking on the phone, we have decided to meet in the place where I was conceived: New York City.

I enter through the double doors. Every seat in the lounge is taken. I scan the crowd for her and try not to panic. I calm my nerves with a self-audit, smoothing my trousers and touching each piece of jewelry: earrings, necklace, wedding ring.

I feel a gloved hand tap my shoulder.

"Madam, are you meeting someone?" the doorman asks.

My breath is loud in my ears. My first instinct is to run—to willfully smile and snap "No" and push back through the double doors into the glaring New York sunset.

But then I feel it. I feel a strangely beautiful gravity pulling me back. Back into the moment. *It's her. I know it's her.* Standing behind me. Waiting. I close my eyes. I take in the feeling. "Madam?" the doorman repeats.

My doubts fall away and leave me weightless and whole. I turn. I look. I see the frame of my face in another's. I see my eyes staring back at me. It's her. It is her. She is lovely. She is delicate. She is a familiar mix of me.

"Kathy," she says, asking yet knowing. Her voice is gentle and perfect. I can only smile in response. She steps toward me. Her open arms pull me in.

And for the first time in my life, I feel the embrace of my mother.

PART XIV

Julie (and Kathy)

Sixty-Two

MOTHER AND DAUGHTER

It's been over four years now since Kathy and I reunited. We have discovered that we are just like most other mothers and daughters—alike yet different, in countless ways. We get along very well. We know that's not always the case when a child and birth mother reunite. Maybe it's working out for us because we waited a while before meeting for the first time. Maybe it's because we were in no hurry and made sure to savor every moment. Maybe it's because we emailed back and forth several times a week and wrote about run-of-the-mill things. Or maybe her adoptive father cherished her in such a way that she became a woman with an open heart, who understands why I gave her up. There is no blame to fuel my guilt.

When we talk on Skype we can see the expressions on each other's faces. She can see my hair uncombed and standing on end and I can see her looking neat and chic. I can see her dog Peaches scratching at the door to be let out, and she can see the framed picture of the Bucks County Playhouse she sent, hanging behind me in my office. I can catch glimpses of Bryan and my granddaughters as they come and go and call out a 'Hello' to them; and she can have a quick chat with Frank when he hears her voice and comes rushing in. Even though we live far away from each other, we can feel the swing and the sway of one another's households.

***

The first time Kathy flew up from Florida to visit us in California, we met her at Bob Hope Airport in Burbank, which is just fifteen minutes from our house, and is the same airport Amelia Earhart used to fly out of. It has been used as a filming location for many movies, including *Giant*, starring Elizabeth Taylor, Rock Hudson and James Dean and *Indiana Jones and the Last Crusade*, starring Harrison Ford and Sean Connery. It was built in the '20s, is surrounded by beautiful hills and looks like it could be in any country in the world. Frank and I got there early by maybe an hour, and when Kathy's plane finally landed we watched with our hearts in our throats as they wheeled the steps over to it, and she descended. Of course, she was the most beautiful person to get off the plane that day.

Our home is big. European style. Burnt yellow with lots of tall asparagus-green French windows. We built it to look as though it had been constructed many years ago, because we love old things—high ceilings, detailed molding and surprise nooks and crannies. Sometimes it feels like a small hotel because it has an elevator in it. Many TV series like *Desperate Housewives* and *Monk* have filmed at the house. Most fun of them all, were the four consecutive years in which the award-winning HBO show, *Entourage*, used it as Ari Gold's house.

Irma, who also kept house for Frank's parents before she came to us, has everything shiny and clean at all times. She is also magical at arranging flowers from our garden and placing them all over the house. Our front garden is filled with olive trees. In the autumn the trees become so overloaded with olives that they fall to the ground en masse and stain our driveway with a lovely soft patina, making it feel like we are living in Italy. In the back, the garden stretches out for over half an acre and consists of shoulder-high hedges that surround beds of wild rosemary, heather and sweet-smelling lavender. Purple wisteria hangs from a balcony and grows up the side of the house, then tumbles down until it almost touches the lawn below. A wandering path of brown pebbles leads to a rose garden and secret paths beyond. Elsewhere, artichoke and hydrangea bushes appear. In the summer we have beds of white impatiens scattered around, and in the winter the same beds are planted with lines and lines of alternating white and purple cabbages. We also have an Olympic-size pool built by Walt Disney, we were told, when he owned the land many years ago. All of this is enclosed by wrought iron gates, which stand at the entrance to our property.

Kathy and I had exchanged pictures of our houses over the year, so we knew that Kathy's small and charming home was not only walking distance to the ocean but also very near to where many world-champion surfers surfed. She knew that our house was large and walking distance to most of the Hollywood studios. After we picked her up from the airport, we took her on a short tour pointing out Warner Bros., Disney and Universal Studios, and a few of our famous neighbors' homes. It was nice taking our time driving around in the cooling afternoon before going directly to the house. Not only were we extremely excited about this visit, but we were very anxious, as well. The fact was, in Frank's and my minds, this was the most important visitor ever to come to our house.

There was also the unspoken fact that, if I had not given Kathy up for adoption some forty-six years before, this would have been her home. Her bedroom would have been one of five on the second floor. Some of her keepsakes would most probably still be on the wall, or set neatly on the table by her bedside, or even hanging in her closet. Could we all three have been thinking the same thing as we finally drove up to the gates for the first time and waited for them to open? This grand Mediterranean Manor could have been the home of Kathy's childhood—but it wasn't.

We had all decided that it would be best to wait until the following day for Kathy to meet her brother and sister and nieces. Again, we wanted to take things slowly, give us all time to adjust to each new moment and avoid being so overwhelmed as to become blind to what *it really felt like* to be just the three of us—Frank, Julie and Kathy, together, for the first time.

The next morning, Frank pleaded for the honor of taking Kathy out on his own. "Just a little time for us to catch up," he promised. So after her hour-long run in and around Toluca Lake, and a quick shower, off they went in Frank's little gray Mercedes, the top down and the voice of Italian singer Laura Pausini filling the late morning air. I watched Kathy sitting next to Frank, her long shiny brown hair blowing in the wind as they headed through the gates, turned left towards Coldwater Canyon and disappeared out of sight. My throat clenched. My heart gave a tug. I fought to catch my breath. *Wait a minute. This wasn't a part of my dream.* Frank and Kathy going off without me; building their own relationship. *What if she likes him more than she likes me?* "Oh my God," I chastised myself. "I'm jealous." I couldn't believe it. Was I really jealous that my daughter would like her father more than she liked me? I was appalled at myself for having these feelings, and embarrassed.

What kind of mother was I? I went inside and closed the front door behind me. *I'm a sixty-four year old mother*, I answered myself. That's what I am. *And by now I'm old enough not to be bamboozled by this petty little millisecond of jealousy.* A lot of birth mothers must feel this way. Not wanting to share their birth child with anyone else, even the child's father. And how difficult it must be for the birth mother who is not married to the birth father. This was just another unexpected jolt along the way. It would be unfair to interfere with the connection they were building. I just had to be aware of my feelings, accept them, laugh a little, and be pleased for the two of them. But still...

Frank gave Kathy a tour of Beverly Hills, then took her to lunch at an outdoor *trattoria.* He told me later that "at the end of lunch she just reached over and picked up the check, smiled at me and said, 'This one's on me, Dad,' and paid for it herself." Frank is the kind of person who picks up checks—not just for his children, but for everyone. He was not accustomed to having someone else pay. "Give a man a fish and you feed him for a day," he told Kathy, trying to finagle the check away from her. "Teach a man to fish and you feed him for a lifetime. I am the kind of father who believes that what you do is give your child a fish every day so the child can eat for a lifetime." "That's not the way I see it," she had told him, holding onto the check tightly and giving him a sweet smile.

Having been left alone to myself turned out not to be such a bad thing. I had the time to work out my new feelings and quietly revel in this new world that was, little by little, opening up to me now that I had Kathy in my life. Also, I had to prepare a big family dinner before they got back. Curry. It is the only thing I really know how to make, and it was what my mother always made for her dinner parties. I have her hand-written recipe, covered in grease spots and smudges. Even though I have it memorized by now, I still take it out when I make it. Her curry takes hours to prepare as the recipe calls for over a dozen different condiments, all of which must be meticulously chopped up and served in separate little bowls on the side. I make her proud each time I make it.

***

Kathy, Frank and I, Frank, Jr., Danielle and James, Martha, then aged fifteen and Irene, twelve, all gathered around our dining table—a long, carved, mahogany antique piece that had once belonged to my great-great-grandfather. Kathy sat next to Danielle and Fran sat on the other side of the table, where he could see the two of them sitting side by side. Frank was at one end of the table, I at the other, and Martha, Irene and James were scattered around in between us all. Conversation normally flows easily between us. Even when the grandchildren were little they were encouraged to talk about anything they wished, and most often did, with great enthusiasm. Usually, after covering the subject of what is new in all of our lives, we automatically move on to talk about books and films. Our family, very polite otherwise, becomes energetic and even boisterous when seated around a table—we interrupt each other to get a point across, let out shrieks of uproarious laughter and shout at the tops of our lungs if we have to. But with Kathy there, our guest of honor that night, all faces were turned toward her, and we were on our best behavior. With hushed voices, so as not to scare or overwhelm her, Danielle, Fran, James and the girls began to ask her questions. "What is your life like?" "What do you do on Saturday evenings?" "Do our cousins surf?" "Do you still surf?" And the most important question of all: "What did you feel when you found out that you not only had a mother and father who were married to each other, but that you had a full brother and sister, too?" Everyone wanted to know everything. Poor Kathy, like the brilliant teacher she is, she took her time and straightforwardly answered all the questions they asked her. From the edge of our chairs we all listened and nodded.

I don't remember who suggested it. I only know that it wasn't me. Suddenly, I was running up to my office on the second floor and searching through my files for the copy of the Non-Identifying Information chart that Kathy had sent me along with her first letter. Grabbing it up, I ran, skipping stairs, back into the dining room. It was Fran (the one in our family most capable of putting two and two together and coming up with twenty hilarious jokes and who would, a few years later, host his own radio show) who reached out for it. After he studied it for a few seconds he began to double over with laughter. No one except Kathy, Frank and I had seen it before. We all looked at him in horror. Then he began to read sections out loud. "Birth Father: Age: 23... Religion: Jewish... Occupation: Actor... Description: 5'6", 150 pounds..." "Five foot six? *I'm* five foot six," Martha interrupted with a whisper. "Grandpa's way taller than that by at least four inches. Why did they say he was so short?" Fran kept going. "Special aptitudes: Singing and dancing..." We all stared at Frank at the head of the table, looking so debonair. "You were a dancer, Grandpa?" Irene burst in. "Like in Broadway shows?" "No, no," Frank said. "I wasn't a dancer."

"Were you a singer?" Danielle asked. "No," Frank laughed. "I was an actor, just an actor. I didn't dance. I didn't sing. I just acted. And when I met your mother I wasn't even an actor anymore. I was a treasurer in the box office. I don't know where they got their information from, but it's all wrong!"

"I've imagined you being 5'6" for the last ten years," Kathy piped in shyly with a grin on her face. "In fact, with the singing and dancing, I though you might even be gay."

"Not that there's anything wrong with that," Fran threw in, quoting Jerry Seinfeld.

"I thought at one point," Kathy went on, "that you might even be Danny DeVito." And then she couldn't help it and started to laugh. She put her hand over her mouth and tried to cover it, but it was out and everyone had heard it. Danielle, sitting next to her, also put her hand up to cover her mouth a second later. Suddenly they looked like mirror images of each other.

After that, the rest of the table began to rock with laughter too. All of us just bent over, our stomachs hurting, we were laughing so hard. Frank, despite the fact that the joke was on him, was in hysterics too. And then, just like that, we were back to being our boisterous old selves, interrupting, screaming out—and this time Kathy was a part of it all, like she had never *not* been. And, as it turns out, she is one of the most excellent interrupters of us all.

"It's you, Mom," she said, when she finally caught her breath. "You're the one who filled out the Non-Identifying Information papers at Catholic Charities."

"Yeah, what were you thinking?" everyone else asked.

"I don't know," I said shaking my head, maybe happier than I had ever been, with my entire family surrounding me at the dining table for the first time in my life. "I have no idea what I was thinking. I must have been out of my mind."

The next day, when Frank, Jr. called to thank us for dinner, his voice was shaking. He was on the verge of tears. "It was too much for me," he said. "Two sisters, exactly alike. Their voices are the same, their laugh is the same. And even worse, when they talk they both gesture with their hands the same way. Kathy is lovely, wonderful, funny and kind. I'm proud she's my sister, but I have to admit, last night blew my mind."

Danielle's comment on our first family dinner together: "Oh my God, I'm a middle child."

I'm not sure how others would have handled the appearance of an older full sister after forty-some years. But I do know that pretty much from the start there was never any question as to whether Danielle or Frank, Jr. would welcome Kathy into our family. I asked them each why this was, and both told me that it was because Kathy finding me had made me so happy. Because they loved me, if having Kathy in my life made me happy, it couldn't help but make them glad.

They have always been compassionate, supportive and loving adults. They are also very intuitive and emotionally attentive people and would never compromise their integrity by forcing themselves to feel something that is not real for the sake of making me happy or for keeping the peace. Yet they are both peacemakers. But I do think it could have gone either way. I know that there must have been times when they were anxious, untrusting and afraid for me. They must have felt possessive of this family, which suddenly, after decades, now had to be shared with someone they'd just met. It can't have been easy—it must have been heart-wrenching, disorienting and a mixture of a thousand other feelings, positive and not. But they are on the other side of that now. They have both included their sister in their lives. She is now one of them. There's no backing away now. Everyone is only going forward.

***

Several months after Kathy's visit to our home, she and I met again in New York City. By then we had decided to write a book together, and we were trying to come up with a title (*Keyword: Adoption, Lost & Found, Cut from the Same Cloth, Separated at Birth,* and *Finding Aimee* were some of our first attempts).

Our first evening together, we talked about what it had been like for her visiting us in Los Angeles. "Your house is gorgeous," she told me. "Everything in it is beautiful. My sister and brother were very lucky to have grown up in it and have all the things that they had. But I have to say, I really loved growing up in my own house, having the things I had, doing the things I did. I loved my family and my schools and my friends. I love my memories, even the bad ones, because they're *my* memories, not anyone else's."

How did I react to that beautiful and honest statement? I simply let out a long breath, and with it came out forty-six years of unadulterated guilt. It was conversations like this one with Kathy, unexpected conversations, frank and open ones, that helped me understand and appreciate the true depth of her—her honesty, her humility and her wisdom. These are not genetic traits. I had nothing to do with any of these qualities. The sound of her voice, her high forehead, the slope of her nose—these had been passed down to her by me. But her profound insightfulness, her unassuming nature, those qualities were not anything I could lay claim to and could only admire and be in awe of.

Frank and I were *both* in awe of her. One day, as father and daughter strolled along the beach on one of our visits to Florida, Kathy had simply said to Frank, "You know, all a daughter wants from her father is for him to be proud of her."

"Look at you," he'd said. "You're an award-winning teacher and the chairman of the English department in a huge high school. You're an incredible mother. You're kind and graceful and good. I could not possibly be prouder."

***

I am as amazed by my four granddaughters, Amanda, Martha, Kathryn and Irene, who are fanciful and funny. They are not afraid of storms, for both of their mothers have taught them how to navigate through rough waters. They all have strong convictions and charmed power. They are rich with imagination. As each of them is different as night is from day, their love reaches out to me in separate and wondrous ways. Danielle's daughters, Martha and Irene, are so much a part of me that I could pick them out of a mob just by breathing in their simple sweet scent. Getting to know Kathy's girls, Amanda and Kathryn, melts my heart because, right from the start, they loved me and included me in their family despite the fact that, really, I was a stranger to them. This was unbelievable to me and totally unexpected. But their constancy inspires me and reminds me of Buddha's words: "Thousands of candles can be lighted from a single candle, and the life of the candle will not be shortened. Happiness never decreases by being shared." And neither does love.

Amanda and Kathryn came West last year to join up with Martha and Irene for three days. One early morning we all went to Malibu to walk along the beach. Barefooted and happy, the wind blowing ocean spray gently against our faces, we stood together wrapped in our sweaters, watching the waves come in and out. And I loved so much at that moment. I loved until it hurt. And then all at once, there was no more hurt. Only love.

Epilogue

KATHY

For my 46th birthday, my birth father invited me to join him on the set of his film, *Revenge of the Bridesmaids*. Little did I know when I stepped off the plane in New Orleans that I had just traversed worlds. He met me in the terminal wearing a navy blue blazer, neatly pressed khaki pants, and a golden smile. After checking me into a suite at the Roosevelt on Baronne Street, we went to Galatoire's in the French Quarter—a restaurant with crisp, white tablecloths and professional waiters, who, after a short conversation about our culinary desires, filled our table with oysters Rockefeller, crabmeat, escargots, and crispy fried frog legs topped with Pernod-infused garlic-herb butter.

The next day we met in the hotel lobby before dawn, ordered a hot cup of coffee to go, and headed to the set. As soon as we pulled up, the transportation coordinator greeted us. "Good morning, Mr. von Zerneck," he smiled. "I'll take your car." He nodded at me as my father handed him the keys.

We walked on set and within minutes were surrounded by actors, the director, cinematographer and crew.

"Frank, I'd like to make a change to today's shooting order."

"Frank, would you mind looking at the angle of this shot?"

"Frank, do you have a minute to review the changes to the script?"

I would have been overwhelmed; I would have sprinted back to the car, driven to the Roosevelt, and hid under the covers until the sun went down. But when I looked over at my father I saw a man, self-assured and alive, with a contagious energy, whose countenance had been long earned by years of well-made decisions. Within minutes, the set was running like a well-oiled machine.

That day I experienced the life that could have been mine, *the life of Aimee*, the life of a respected executive producer's daughter. I sat behind the camera in a director's chair, I played an extra in a poignant scene, I ate lunch with the cast and I carefully watched the dailies with everyone. And I felt as if I belonged.

I was sad to see that week come to an end. During those few days I experienced a life very foreign to me. A life as my father's daughter.

***

In early 2008, I bought tickets to the musical *Camelot*, starring Lou Diamond Phillips. "You should go backstage and meet Lou after the show," my sister Danielle suggested over the phone. "Tell him our story." During the filming of *La Bamba* in the late '80s, Danielle, who played Donna and Lou, who played Richie Valens, had become friends. "I haven't seen him in years; please tell him I say hello."

After the performance I went backstage to introduce myself. He was surrounded by a string of local radio and television personalities holding small microphones waiting for the chance to interview him. I stood back in the hallway, just outside his dressing room door, waiting, like the others, for my turn. I could see his chiseled features smiling graciously as he answered questions from three or four journalists at a time. Then, quite suddenly, he politely threw up his hands and stopped the interviews. "Excuse me," he said. "I'd like to say hello to an old friend." He pushed past the line of people in his dressing room and came out into the hallway with a warm smile and his arms outstretched.

"Danielle—" he said as he stepped toward me. But just before he reached in to hug me, he stopped. "Oh, I'm sorry, I thought you were—" he pulled back, perplexed.

"I'm Danielle's sister," I said as I held out my hand and smiled.

This exchange with Lou Diamond Phillips was, for me, exhilarating—not because he was a famous actor whom I'd always hoped I'd meet. It was affecting because, on the most basic of levels, it was an affirmation of the root of my existence. There was someone in this world whom I resembled so strongly that I could be mistaken for her.

Danielle and I don't just look like one another; we share the same laugh, the same intonation of voice, the same sideways tilt of our heads when we speak in earnest. And after spending time with her, I have also realized the semblance resonating on a much deeper level. I saw it when she spoke about politics, about literature, about her daughters; I saw a passion, a fire in her belly, a glimpse of what made her tick—and understood it immediately. We, though strangers, had been cut from the same cloth—and I felt the same thing that other biological siblings must feel—an unspoken connection.

My relationships with Danielle and Frank, who have graciously shared their parents with me, have been the icing on a cake so sweet and incredibly rich that I must be careful not to eat it all at once. I've had to learn to pull back and to allow my siblings the time to get used to the idea of having me as their older sister.

***

On the day I found out my mother was coming to visit me in Florida for the very first time, I was overjoyed. But I was also concerned that I would not measure up. I had wanted this from the beginning—a chance to spend time with her in my home, with my family. I envisioned the two of us sipping our morning cups of coffee at the breakfast table, taking long walks along the beach in the afternoons, and preparing a meal together each evening. But I had been to my parents' home—a home that could comfortably fit ten of mine inside it—and I now wondered whether my breakfast table was too small or if the sidewalks on my street were too uneven.

I spent the weeks before her visit dusting every lampshade and reorganizing every closet. I bought new bath towels, steam-cleaned the bedroom carpets, and planted a bed of yellow petunias outside the kitchen window. On my way to the airport to pick her up, all I could think about was the fact that I had forgotten to clean the guest bathroom mirror. I was a nervous wreck. But that all melted away the second she threw her arms around me—arms that were so good at "disarming" me, arms that, with one touch, told me I *did* measure up. Not because of the size of my home or the orderliness of my closets, but because I was someone of whom she was proud; I was someone whom she loved; I was someone special—her daughter.

It wasn't until that week, the week spent with my mother in my own home, that I had a greater sense of what I had missed out on. She spent time with my daughters, painting their nails and playing Apples to Apples. She fawned over each dish I served: the waffles, the stromboli, the strawberries dipped in sour cream and brown sugar. She went fishing with Bryan. After that week, I realized how fortunate I was to have this remarkable woman in my life, a woman who had slowly, gently, lovingly threaded herself into the fabric of *my* family.

***

The process of reuniting with my birth family has resulted in the discovery of some interesting parallels. For example, both of my fathers, adoptive and natural, are named Frank. This is also true of my brothers. Another coincidence I found intriguing is that both of my fathers had the same telephone number for much of their lives—different area codes, of course.

The first time I called my birth father's cell phone, the name that appeared on it was that of my adoptive mother, Kathy Conway. Our phones are all in Bryan's name and Kathy Conway does not appear anywhere in our accounts. Yet, here was her name, and, here, I believe, was she, giving me her blessing. I think most adoptees feel a sense of disloyalty when they reach out to reunite with their birth parents. I know I have. But each synchronicity feels like a permission slip to move forward. I'm grateful for these para-llels, as they have helped me form a bond with my birth family that otherwise may have been stymied by guilt.

We have taken our time getting to know one another. Our relationship has had the luxury of a gestation period—a block of time that nature affords to every mother and her offspring. Taking things slowly has allowed time for our emotions to catch up with our newfound reality. And, in the words of the poet Robert Frost, "...that has made all the difference."

JULIE

Two summers ago Kathy and I traveled to Paris together. On our first day there we went to Notre Dame, where, side-by-side, we lit long, narrow candles. And blessed ourselves. I love restaurants and enjoy a glass of red wine, especially when I'm in Paris. Kathy, however, does not like restaurants. And she seldom drinks. So, we ended up buying fresh baguettes and cheeses and fruit and sparkling water from small markets and picnicking in parks like the Luxembourg and the Tuileries Gardens. Our favorite park was a very small one on Rue du Bac, where we went almost every afternoon and sat on green benches and watched the children play. We had a grand time together. Mostly we walked and talked. And laughed. In the early mornings we walked along the Seine and watched the booksellers set up their stalls and lay out their goods. In the late afternoons we pushed our way through crowded Metro stations and were awed by the music of musicians that echoed in the tunnels along the way, entire bands sometimes, and sometimes a single beguiling accordion. Some nights we wandered the narrow, slick and shiny cobblestone streets, in the rain, pressed together under one black umbrella held high over both our heads.

One afternoon Kathy bought herself a great big straw hat in the square at the Place des Vosges to keep the sun out of her eyes, and I took a dozen pictures of her in it.

There we were. Together. Two people who had been strangers for most of their lives.

Imagine that. Me—taking a picture of the daughter I gave up. She—smiling at me from under her hat. In Paris. On a sunny day.

One of the dozen photos of Kathy taken in Paris

ABOVE: Julie and Frank with Kathy in their favorite LA restaurant, *Firenze Osteria*
BELOW: Julie and Kathy in Orlando, Florida, 2011

ABOVE: Frank meeting Kathy at Burbank Airport for her first visit to LA
BELOW: Julie and Kathy, in Toluca Lake, California, writing *Secret Storms*

ABOVE: Danielle, Kathy, and Frank, Jr. in Toluca Lake, California
BELOW: Kathy on the set of *Revenge of the Bridesmaids* in New Orleans

Julie and Kathy having a meal on yet another park bench in Paris

ABOVE: Kathryn, Amanda, Martha, and Irene at the beach together in Los Angeles
BELOW: Frank, Jr., Danielle, Kathy, with their mother and father

ACKNOWLEDGMENTS

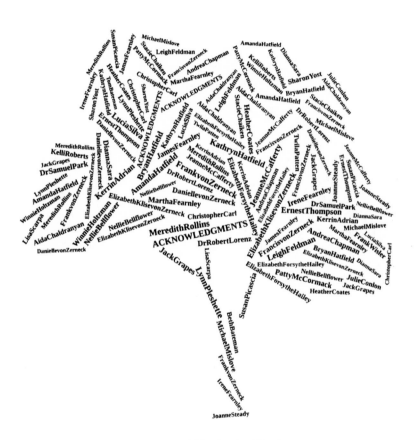

Special Thanks to David Rawle

Kathy Hatfield was born in Philadelphia, Pennsylvania, and grew up surrounded by two brothers, twenty-five cousins, and two sets of grandparents in Indialantic, Florida. She attended Florida Atlantic University, after which she worked as a mortgage broker while running her own small business selling men's neckties. She now teaches World Literature at a high school in Florida where she serves as English department chairman. She and her husband of 25 years live in a quaint beachside community with their two daughters. She is a freelance writer and moderator of the Adoption Reunion Stories Facebook page, which currently has over 2,800 members. She's a competitive runner and participates in 5k races when she's not correcting papers.

Julie Mannix von Zerneck was born in Bryn Mawr, Pennsylvania. She traveled with her parents, living in Paris, on the isle of Capri and in several boarding schools around the world, before settling down at Sunny Hill Farm at the age of nine. There, she lived with a menagerie of animals, including a cheetah and eagle and her very own baby spider monkey. After attending the Neighborhood Playhouse in NYC, she became an actress on Broadway, had running roles in three soap operas and guest starred on many TV series. She is married to the TV producer, Frank von Zerneck. They have three children and four grandchildren and reside in Toluca Lake, California, where, for 26 wonderful years, they were the owners of Portrait of a Bookstore. She is a lifelong collector of antiques and antiquarian books.

CPSIA information can be obtained at www.ICGtesting.com
Printed in the USA
LVOW06s2155151213

365463LV00002B/153/P